Study Guide for the *Music* Tests:

Concepts and Processes; Analysis; and *Content Knowledge*

► ► ► ► ► ► ► ► ► ► ► ►

A PUBLICATION OF EDUCATIONAL TESTING SERVICE

Acknowledgements

Educational Testing Service and The Praxis Series™ wish to extend special thanks to the following for helping with this publication as part of their commitment to promoting music education:

- Margaret A. Wang, Director of Professional Development, MENC: The National Association for Music Education.

- Debbie Lynn Wolf, Ph.D., Chair of the Music Education Program in the School of Music and Performing Arts at Philadelphia Biblical University, Director of the PBU Community School of Music, and a chief reader of the ETS Praxis Exams.

- Classic Produktion Osnabrück (CPO), Lübecker Str. 9, D-49124 Georgmarienhütte, Germany

- Hyperion Records, PO Box 25, London SE9 1AX, England

Table of Contents

Study Guide for the *Music* Tests

► ► ► ► ► ► ► ► ► ► ► ►

TABLE OF CONTENTS

Chapter 1

Introduction to the *Music* Tests and Suggestions for Using this Study Guide 7

Chapter 2

Background Information on The Praxis Series™ Assessments 13

The *Music: Content Knowledge* Test

Chapter 3

Preparing for the *Music: Content Knowledge* Test 17

Chapter 4

Don't be Defeated by Multiple-Choice Questions 35

Chapter 5

Practice Test, *Music: Content Knowledge* 47

Chapter 6

Right Answers and Explanations for the *Music: Content Knowledge* Test 75

The Constructed-Response Tests in *Music*

Chapter 7

Constructed-Response Tests and How Your Responses Will Be Scored 85

The *Music: Concepts and Processes* Test

Chapter 8

Preparing for the *Music: Concepts and Processes* Test 95

Chapter 9

Practice Test, *Music: Concepts and Processes* 115

Chapter 10

Sample Responses to Question 1A of *Music: Concepts and Processes* and
How They Were Scored 127

Chapter 11

Sample Responses to Question 1B of *Music: Concepts and Processes* and How They Were Scored 139

Chapter 12

Sample Responses to Question 2 of *Music: Concepts and Processes* and How They Were Scored 153

The *Music: Analysis* Test

Chapter 13

Preparing for the *Music: Analysis* Test 165

Chapter 14

Practice Test, *Music: Analysis* 171

Chapter 15

Sample Responses to *Music: Analysis* and How They Were Scored 187

Chapter 16

Are You Ready? Last-Minute Tips 203

Appendix A

Study Plan Sheet 207

Appendix B

For More Information 209

Appendix C

Index Numbers on the Enclosed CD 211

Appendix D

List of Resources 213

Appendix E

Recorded Excerpts 221

Appendix F

Response Space for the *Music: Analysis* Test 225

Chapter 1

Introduction to the *Music* Tests and Suggestions for Using this Study Guide

► ► ► ► ► ► ► ► ► ► ► ►

Introduction to the *Music* Tests

The Praxis *Music* tests assess beginning teachers' understanding of the essential content of undergraduate music and music education courses. Educational Testing Service (ETS) has selected the content of this test using resources such as the National Standards for Education in the Arts and the NAEP Arts Education Assessment Framework. ETS also refers to current practices as specified by national music educator institutions and organizations such as MENC: The National Association for Music Education. In developing assessment material for these tests, ETS works in collaboration with teacher educators, higher education content specialists, and accomplished practicing teachers to keep the test updated and representative of current standards.

There are currently three different Praxis *Music* tests:

- *Music: Content Knowledge* (0113)
- *Music: Concepts and Processes* (0111)
- *Music: Analysis* (0112)

The *Music: Content Knowledge* test (0113) consists of 135 multiple-choice questions. The first 40 questions are paced by a CD that contains the musical excerpts for these questions. You must complete these questions in approximately 45 minutes, which is how long the CD plays. You then have approximately 75 minutes to answer the remaining 95 questions. Thus, a total of two hours is available for completing the test.

The questions cover five major areas, in the following proportions:

Content Categories	Approximate Number of Questions	Approximate Percentage of Examination
Music History and Literature	28*	21%
Music Theory	28*	21%
Performance	28*	21%
Music Learning, K-12	43	31%
Professional Practices	8	6%
*About half of these questions are based on recorded excerpts.		

The *Music: Concepts and Processes* test (0111) consists of two questions, each of which counts for 50 percent of your test score. One question requires you to describe an instructional sequence focusing on a specific musical concept as it would be taught to a general music class. The other question covers teaching individual and ensemble performance techniques. You are given a choice of either instrumental or choral music topics and have one hour to complete the test. You are advised to pace yourself so that you can give sufficient attention to both questions.

 TIP

This is not a test of your writing ability. A response in an essay format is not required. You may use short descriptions or phrases, as long as your ideas are clear and you support your ideas with relevant examples and details where appropriate.

The *Music: Analysis* test (0112) consists of three questions, and you have one hour to complete the test. The first two questions present you with two brief musical scores: one for an instrumental chamber ensemble and the other for a choral ensemble. For each score, a recording of a musical performance is played and you are asked to identify errors—that is, departures from the score as written. The errors may include the following:

- imbalance among instruments or voices
- incorrect accents
- incorrect articulation
- incorrect interpretation of dynamic or tempo markings

You are not expected to identify errors in pitch, rhythm, or diction. ***Note:*** *The errors heard in the recordings are flagrant performance mistakes of the kinds you would expect students to make. You are not required to discern subtle nuances or judge subjective matters of interpretation.* You have approximately 30 minutes to answer the first two questions, and each accounts for approximately 25 percent of your test score.

The third question for the *Music: Analysis* test covers score analysis, with a choice of instrumental, choral, and general music. You are presented with two brief excerpts from printed musical scores and are required to do the following:

- choose a suitable grade level and/or ensemble type for each musical score
- identify stylistic influences in the excerpts
- identify and describe significant performance challenges or music concepts represented by the excerpts
- describe rehearsal techniques that would help students meet performance challenges, or explain how the excerpts could be used to teach music concepts

You have approximately 30 minutes to answer the third question, and it accounts for approximately 50 percent of your test score.

TIP

This is not a test of your writing ability. A response in an essay format is not required. You may use short descriptions or phrases, as long as your ideas are clear and you support your ideas with relevant examples and details where appropriate.

How to Use This Study Guide

Q. Why should you use this study guide?

This test is different from a final exam or other tests you may have taken for other courses because it is comprehensive—that is, it covers material you may have learned in several courses during your entire undergraduate program. It requires you to synthesize information you have learned from many sources and to understand the subject as a whole.

Therefore, you should review and prepare for it, rather than merely becoming familiar with the question formats. A thorough review of the material covered on the test will significantly increase your likelihood of success. Moreover, studying for your licensing exam is a great opportunity to reflect on and develop a deeper understanding of musical and pedagogical knowledge and methods before you begin to teach or to reflect on previous teaching experience. As you prepare to take the test, it may be particularly helpful for you to think about how you would apply the study topics and sample exercises to the clinical experience you obtained during your teacher preparation program. Your student teaching experience will be especially relevant to your thinking about the materials in the study guide.

Q. How can you best use the "Study Topics" chapter of this study guide?

(Note: This section applies only to the *Music: Content Knowledge* test [0113].)

First, assess your current knowledge and use that assessment to complete your preparation and review for the test.

- **Become familiar with the test content.** Learn what will be tested, as covered in chapter 3.
- **Assess how well you know the content in each area.** After you learn what topics the test contains, you should assess your knowledge in each area. How well do you know the material? In which areas do you need to learn more before you take the test? It is quite likely that you will need to brush up on most or all of the areas.
- **Develop a study plan.** Assess what you need to study and create a realistic plan for studying. You can develop your study plan in any way that works best for you. A "Study Plan" form is included in appendix A at the end of the book as a possible way to structure your planning. Remember that you will need to allow time to find books, CDs, and other materials, time to read and listen to the materials and take notes, and time to apply your learning to the practice questions.
- **Identify study materials.** Most of the material covered by the test is contained in standard textbooks in the field. If you no longer own the texts you used in your undergraduate course work, you may want to borrow some from friends or from a library. Use standard textbooks and other reliable, professionally prepared materials. Don't rely heavily on information provided by friends or from searching the World Wide Web. Neither of these sources is as uniformly reliable as textbooks.
- **Work through your study plan.** You may want to work alone, or you may find it more helpful to work with a group or with a mentor. Work through the topics and questions provided in chapter 3. Rather than memorizing definitions from books, be able to define and discuss the topics in your own words and understand the relationships between diverse topics and concepts. If you are working with a group or mentor, you can also try informal quizzes and questioning techniques.

- **Proceed to the practice questions.** Once you have completed your review, you are ready to benefit from the "Practice Questions" portion of this guide.

Q. What's the best way to use the chapter on multiple-choice questions?

(Note: This section applies only to the *Music: Content Knowledge* test [0113].)

Read chapter 4. This chapter will sharpen your skills in reading and answering multiple-choice questions. For you to succeed on multiple-choice questions, you must focus carefully on the question, avoid reading things into the question, pay attention to details, and sift patiently through the answer choices.

Q. What's the best way to prepare for a constructed-response test with this study guide?

(Note: This section applies only to the *Music: Concepts and Processes* [0111] and *Music: Analysis* [0112] tests.)

- **Understand how constructed-response tests are scored.** Read chapter 7 to understand how the scoring process works for these tests and to see specifically what the test scorers will be looking for when they evaluate your responses.
- **Become familiar with the test content.** Learn what will be tested, as covered in chapters 8 and 13.
- **Assess how well you know the content in each area.** After you learn what topics the test contains, you should assess your knowledge in each area. How well do you know the material? In which areas do you need to learn more before you take the test? It is quite likely that you will need to brush up on most or all of the areas.
- **Develop a study plan.** Assess what you need to study and create a realistic plan for studying. You can develop your study plan in any way that works best for you. A "Study Plan" form is included in appendix A at the end of the book as a possible way to structure your planning. Remember that you will need to allow time to find books, CDs, and other materials, time to read and listen to the materials and take notes, and time to apply your learning to the practice questions.
- **Identify study materials.** Most of the material covered by the test is contained in standard textbooks in the field. If you no longer own the texts you used in your undergraduate coursework, you may want to borrow some from friends or from a library. Use standard textbooks and other reliable, professionally prepared materials. Don't rely heavily on information provided by friends or from searching the World Wide Web. Neither of these sources is as uniformly reliable as textbooks.
- **Work through your study plan.** You may want to work alone, or you may find it more helpful to work with a group or with a mentor. Work through the topics and questions provided in chapter 3. Rather than memorizing definitions from books, be able to define and discuss the topics in your own words and understand the relationships between diverse topics and concepts. If you are working with a group or mentor, you can also try informal quizzes and questioning techniques.
- **Sharpen your skills on short-answer questions.** Read chapters 8 and 13 to understand how short-answer questions are scored and how to write high-scoring responses.
- **Proceed to the practice questions.** Once you have completed your review, you are ready to benefit from the "Practice Questions" portion of this guide.

Q. What's the best way to use the practice-test chapters?

- **Answer the short-answer questions.** Work on the practice cases and short-answer questions (chapter 9 for *Concepts and Processes*, or chapter 14 for *Analysis*), then review the scoring materials and sample responses (chapters 10, 11, and 12 for *Concepts and Processes*, or chapter 15 for *Analysis*).
- **Answer the practice multiple-choice questions.** Work on the practice multiple-choice questions in chapter 5, then use chapter 6 to mark the questions you answered correctly and the ones you missed. In chapter 6 also look over the explanations of the questions you missed and see whether you understand them.
- **Decide whether you need more review.** After you have looked at your results, decide whether there are areas that you need to brush up on before taking the actual test. Go back to your textbooks and reference materials to see whether the topics are covered there. You may also want to go over your questions with a friend or teacher who is familiar with the subjects.
- **Assess your readiness.** Do you feel confident about your level of understanding in each of the subject areas? If not, where do you need more work? If you feel ready, complete the checklist in chapter 16 to double-check that you've thought through the details. If you need more information about registration or the testing situation itself, use the resources in appendix B, "For More Information."

Chapter 2

Background Information on The Praxis Series™ Assessments

► ► ► ► ► ► ► ► ► ► ► ►

What Are The Praxis Series™ Subject Assessments?

The Praxis Series™ Subject Assessments are designed by Educational Testing Service (ETS) to assess your knowledge of the subject area you plan to teach, and they are a part of the licensing procedure in many states. This study guide covers an assessment that tests your knowledge of the actual content you hope to be licensed to teach. Your state has adopted The Praxis Series tests because it wants to be certain that you have achieved a specified level of mastery of your subject area before it grants you a license to teach in a classroom.

The Praxis Series tests are part of a national testing program, meaning that the test covered in this study guide is used in more than one state. The advantage of taking Praxis tests is that if you want to teach in another state that uses The Praxis Series tests, you can transfer your scores to that state. Passing scores are set by states, however, so if you are planning to apply for licensure in another state, you may find that passing scores are different. You can find passing scores for all states that use The Praxis Series tests on-line at **www.ets.org/praxis/prxstate.html** or in the *Understanding Your Praxis Scores* pamphlet, available either in your college's School of Education or by calling 609-771-7395.

What Is Licensure?

Licensure in any area—medicine, law, architecture, accounting, cosmetology—is an assurance to the public that the person holding the license has demonstrated a certain level of competence. The overriding concept behind licensure is expressed in the commonly used phrase that the person holding the license *will do no harm*. In the case of teacher licensing, a license tells the public that the person holding the license can be trusted to educate children competently and professionally.

Because a license makes such a serious claim about its holder, licensure tests are usually quite demanding. In some fields, licensure tests have more than one part and last for more than one day. Test takers for licensure in all fields plan intensive study as part of their professional preparation: some join study groups, others study alone. But preparing to take a licensure test is, in all cases, a professional activity. Because it assesses your entire body of knowledge or skill for the field you want to enter, preparing for a licensure exam takes planning, discipline, and sustained effort. Studying thoroughly is highly recommended.

Why Does My State Require The Praxis Series Assessments?

Your state chose The Praxis Series Assessments because the tests assess the breadth and depth of content—called the "domain" of the test—that your state wants its teachers to possess before they begin to teach. The level of content knowledge, reflected in the passing score, is based on recommendations of panels of teachers and teacher educators in each subject area in each state. The state licensing agency and, in some states, the state legislature, ratify the passing scores that have been recommended by panels of teachers. You can find out the passing score required for The Praxis Series Assessments in your state by looking in the pamphlet *Understanding Your Praxis Scores*, which is free from ETS (see above). If you look through this pamphlet, you will see that not all states use the same test modules, and even when they do, the passing scores can differ from state to state.

What Kinds of Tests Are The Praxis Series Subject Assessments?

Two kinds of tests comprise The Praxis Series Subject Assessments: multiple choice (for which you select your answer from a list of choices) and constructed response (for which you write a response of your own). Multiple-choice tests can survey a wider domain because they can ask more questions in a limited period of time. Constructed-response tests have far fewer questions, but the questions require you to demonstrate the depth of your knowledge in the area covered.

What Do the Tests Measure?

The Praxis Series Subject Assessments are tests of content knowledge. They measure your understanding of the subject area you want to teach. The multiple-choice tests measure a broad range of knowledge across your content area. The constructed-response tests measure your ability to explain in depth a few essential topics in your subject area. The content-specific pedagogy tests, most of which are constructed response, measure your understanding of how to teach certain fundamental concepts in your field. The tests do not measure your actual teaching ability, however. They measure your knowledge of the subject and of how to teach it. The teachers in your field who help us design and write these tests, and the states that require these tests, do so in the belief that knowledge of a subject area is the first requirement for licensing. Your teaching ability is a skill that is measured in other ways: Observation, videotaped teaching, or portfolios are typically used by states to measure teaching ability. Teaching combines many complex skills, only some of which can be measured by a single test. The Praxis Series Subject Assessments are designed to measure how thoroughly you understand the material in the subject areas in which you want to be licensed to teach.

How Were These Tests Developed?

ETS began the development of The Praxis Series Subject Assessments with a survey. For each subject, teachers around the country in various teaching situations were asked to judge which knowledge and skills a beginning teacher in that subject needs to possess. Professors in schools of education who prepare teachers were asked the same questions. These responses were ranked in order of importance and sent out to hundreds of teachers for review. All of the responses to these surveys (called "job analysis surveys") were analyzed to summarize the judgments of these professionals. From their consensus, we developed the specifications for the multiple-choice and constructed-response tests. For each subject area, a committee of practicing teachers and teacher educators wrote these specifications (guidelines). The specifications were reviewed and eventually approved by teachers. From the test specifications, groups of teachers and professional test developers created test questions.

When your state adopted The Praxis Series Subject Assessments, local panels of practicing teachers and teacher educators in each subject area met to examine the tests question by question and evaluate each question for its relevance to beginning teachers in your state. This process is known as a "validity study." A test is considered "valid" for a job if it measures what people must know and be able to do on that job. For the test to be adopted in your state, teachers in your state must judge that it is valid.

These teachers and teacher educators also performed a "standard-setting study"; that is, they went through the tests question by question and decided, through a rigorous process, how many questions a beginning teacher should be able to answer correctly. From this study emerged a recommended passing score. The final passing score was approved by your state's Department of Education.

In other words, throughout the development process, practitioners in the teaching field—teachers and teacher educators—have determined what the tests would contain. The practitioners in your state determined which tests would be used for licensure in your subject area and helped decide what score would be needed to achieve licensure. This is how professional licensure works in most fields: those who are already licensed oversee the licensing of new practitioners. When you pass The Praxis Series Subject Assessments, you and the practitioners in your state can be assured that you have the knowledge required to begin practicing your profession.

Chapter 3

Preparing for the *Music: Content Knowledge* Test

► ► ► ► ► ► ► ► ► ► ► ►

The Praxis *Music: Content Knowledge* test consists of 135 multiple-choice questions administered during a two-hour period. It focuses on the knowledge, skills, and abilities that are important for all beginning music teachers to have. Many of the questions focus on the comprehension and application of concepts, principles, and practices. Forty of the questions are based on musical excerpts recorded on a CD and played for examinees in the test center.

The approximate content emphasis is as follows.

- Basic Musicianship (History and Literature, Theory, Performance): 63%
- Music Learning, K–12: 31%
- Professional Practices: 6%

This test is used in several states to license K–12 music educators. Licensed educators will teach band, orchestra, chorus, jazz, or general music. That means that there is a wide variety of material represented on the test. This is because states requiring Praxis *Music* examinations typically have standards that reflect the value of comprehensive musicianship; that is, that music education professionals in one specialty should have some familiarity with the materials and practices of the other specialties.

On the other hand, you are *not* expected to be an expert in all of the specialties. Keenly aware that many of the subtopics may lie outside your specialty, the states set passing scores that take this into account. To put it another way, don't be surprised and disturbed if you run into a question on a topic outside your specialty. If you don't know the answer, mark it, come back to it later, and make your best guess.

Overview of Topics

Here is an overview of the topics covered on the test, along with their subtopics. On each test, you will typically find a number of questions on each of the subtopics described in the bulleted items.

History and Literature

- Identification of style characteristics (e.g., melody, rhythm, harmony, texture, instrumentation, and expressive devices) associated with the music of the major historical periods (Medieval, Renaissance, Baroque, Classical, Romantic, twentieth/twenty-first century) and with jazz, other American popular music, and world musics
- Identification of composers based on excerpts (recorded and/or printed) of music
- Identification of various genres and distinguishing between them
- Identification and knowledge of performers (e.g., American jazz musicians)
- Identification of countries or regions of origin for excerpts of world music heard on tape

Theory

- Concepts related to pitch (e.g., scales and scale types, modes, tonality, and harmony)
- Concepts related to rhythm, including meter and durational values
- Musical form and analysis, including large-scale form (such as binary, theme and variations, fugue) and smaller formal structures (such as phrase structure, melodic or rhythmic motives)
- Identification of formal organization of musical excerpts
- Identification and understanding of musical texture (e.g., monophony, homophony, polyphony, imitation)
- Identification and understanding of the use of expressive devices (e.g., dynamics, articulation, tempo, and timbre)
- Identification of compositional elements such as intervals, chords, scales, and rhythmic and melodic patterns in recorded excerpts

Performance

- Identification of musical instruments on recorded excerpts
- Identification of vocal types (e.g., soprano, alto, tenor, bass, coloratura) and vocal techniques from recorded excerpts
- Knowledge of musical instruments, including instrumentation of standard ensembles, basic principles of orchestration, methods of sound production, instrumental techniques, and families of instruments
- Knowledge of the singing voice, including voicing of standard ensembles and principles of good vocal production
- Knowledge of music that combines instruments and voices
- Basic knowledge of electronic instruments (e.g., synthesizers, computers, MIDI)
- Basic understanding of acoustics, especially as it applies to performance situations
- Understanding of conducting skills and concepts
- Facility with score reading (e.g., transposing instruments, interpretation of notation and symbols, and stylistic interpretation) based on printed excerpts of music
- Basic knowledge of improvisation and improvisational techniques, including jazz improvisation
- Identification of errors in performance on recorded excerpts with reference to correctly printed scores

Music Learning, K–12

- Course offerings in general and overall music program objectives as related to accepted standards
- Knowledge of basic requirements in terms of facilities, course offerings, scheduling, staffing, materials and equipment as related to accepted standards
- Curriculum planning and development appropriate for a beginning teacher
- Scope as related to course content, including psychomotor, cognitive, and affective behaviors, and music concepts and elements
- Learning sequences
- Appropriate performance skills for each grade level
- Methods of teaching singing in general music
- Vocal and instrumental literature appropriate for performance by students in grades K–12
- Methods of evaluation and assessment
- Familiarity with the basic principles of pedagogical approaches, such as Orff, Kodály, Dalcroze, and Suzuki
- Music instruction for special and/or gifted students
- Basic knowledge of equipment and technology for the music classroom, including computers, MIDI, and CD-ROM
- Classroom management skills appropriate to the music classroom or student ensemble rehearsal

Professional Practices

- Basic knowledge of the philosophy of music education
- Knowledge of journals, reference works, and other source materials dealing with music education, music literature, performance, history, and theory
- Professional ethics, especially with regard to U.S. copyright law and appropriate venus for performance by student ensembles
- Knowledge of professional organizations, including their philosophies and goals

How to Prepare

In general, there are two effective study strategies. One is to begin with *the things that you know always give you trouble*—the things on which you are weak. Another method is to start with *the things you do best* in order to maximize your potential to score high in areas most comfortable to you. In either case, it is probably best to study both kinds of things at some point in your preparation. The choice of strategy, plus the emphasis you give to each subtopic, is up to you.

The content and difficulty level of the questions mirror the content of a typical four-year, high-quality undergraduate program in music. In accordance with sound assessment practice, the questions run the gamut from easy to difficult. To prepare effectively, you will have to be very honest with yourself about how much you remember and how serious you were in your studies. Now is the time to find your old textbooks and review them thoroughly.

To help prepare for the *Music: Content Knowledge* test, you might use as a study outline the bulleted items given on the previous page. As an example, take a closer look at each bulleted item under **Music History and Literature.** You will want to know as much as you can about . . .

these topics:	**in relation to these periods/styles:**
melody	Medieval
rhythm	Renaissance
harmony	Baroque
texture	Classical
expressive devices (e.g., dynamics, tempo changes)	Romantic
	Twentieth/twenty-first century
representative composers	Jazz
representative works	American popular music
	World music

Special Questions Marked with Stars

Interspersed throughout the list of topics on the following pages are questions that are placed in boxes and preceded by stars (★). These questions are intended to help you test your knowledge of fundamental concepts and your ability to apply fundamental concepts to situations in the real world. Most of the questions require you to combine several pieces of knowledge in order to formulate an integrated understanding and response. If you spend time on these questions, you will gain increased understanding and facility with the subject matter covered on the test. You might want to discuss these questions and your answers with a teacher or mentor.

Note that the questions marked with stars are not short-answer or multiple-choice and that this study guide does not provide the answers. The questions marked with stars are intended as *study* questions, not practice questions. Thinking about the answers to them should improve your understanding of fundamental concepts and will probably help you answer a broad range of questions on the test.

Ideas for Subtopics to Study

Music History and Literature

- Style characteristics
  - Melody
  - Rhythm
  - Harmony
  - Texture
  - Instrumentation
  - Expressive devices

★ Given a recorded musical excerpt, can you identify the major characteristics of the style?

- Major historical periods associated with style characteristics
  - Medieval
  - Renaissance
  - Baroque
  - Classical
  - Romantic
  - Twentieth/twenty-first century

★ Given a recorded musical excerpt, can you identify the time period when it was composed?

- Other musical traditions associated with these
  - Jazz
  - Other American popular music
  - World musics
- Ability to identify historical period and genre of musical examples

★ Given a recorded musical excerpt, can you identify the major characteristics of the style?

★ What was a major influence on the style of the excerpt?

- The unique characteristics of various popular musical styles; ability to recognize recorded excerpts
  - Bebop
  - Blues
  - Dixieland
  - Gospel
  - Motown
  - Ragtime
  - Rap
  - Rhythm and blues
  - Swing

★ Given a recorded musical excerpt in one of these styles, can you identify the style?

- Composers (the following is not intended as a complete list); ability to recognize representative excerpts of their music
  - Milton Babbitt
  - J.S. Bach
  - Béla Bartók
  - Ludwig van Beethoven
  - Alban Berg
  - Hector Berlioz
  - Johannes Brahms
  - Anton Bruckner
  - Elliot Carter
  - Aaron Copland
  - Frédéric Chopin
  - Claude Debussy
  - Guillaume Dufay
  - Edward Elgar

- George Gershwin
- Philip Glass
- Christoph Gluck
- George Handel
- Howard Hanson
- Franz Joseph Haydn
- Gustav Holst
- Hildegard von Bingen
- Charles Ives
- Libby Larsen
- Orlando di Lasso
- Gustav Mahler
- Olivier Messiaen
- Claudio Monteverdi
- W. A. Mozart
- Thea Musgrave
- Palestrina
- Krzysztof Penderecki
- Pérotin
- Giacomo Puccini
- Sergey Rachmaninoff
- Jean-Philippe Rameau
- Maurice Ravel
- Arnold Schoenberg
- Franz Schubert
- William Schuman
- Robert Schumann
- Heinrich Schütz
- Dmitri Shostakovich
- Bedrich Smetana
- William Grant Still
- Richard Strauss
- Igor Stravinsky
- Pyotr Ilich Tchaikovsky
- Joan Tower
- Giuseppe Verdi
- Antonio Vivaldi
- Richard Wagner
- Anton Webern
- Ellen Taaffe Zwilich

★ Who composed *Prelude to the Afternoon of a Faun?*

★ What were some important compositions of Richard Strauss?

★ Given a recorded musical excerpt from a work of Antonio Vivaldi, can you identify the composer?

★ What is the name for the numbering scheme used to categorize Mozart's works?

- Characteristics of various genres
  - Aria
  - Bourrée
  - Cantata
  - Chanson
  - Chorale
  - Chorale prelude
  - Concerto
  - Divertimento
  - Étude
  - Fanfare
  - Fugue
  - Gavotte
  - Gigue
  - Madrigal
  - Motet
  - Opera
  - Organum
  - Passacaglia
  - Recitative
  - Rondeau
  - Sarabande
  - Sonata
  - Song cycle
  - String quartet
  - Suite
  - Symphonic poem
  - Symphony
  - Toccata

★ Describe the differences between the madrigal and motet.

★ Describe the differences between the fugue and the toccata.

★ Given a recorded musical excerpt, can you identify the genre?

- Chronology of composers, excerpts of major literature, and musical styles

★ Compile a timeline of the historical periods, general styles, major composers, typical genre, and specific works.

★ Given a historical period, can you name a representative work?

★ Given an excerpt of popular music, can you describe its relationship to and influences from older styles?

- Performers and their performance styles
  - Louis Armstrong
  - John Coltrane
  - Miles Davis
  - Benny Goodman
  - Peggy Lee
  - Wynton Marsalis
  - Thelonious Monk
  - Charlie Parker
  - Bessie Smith
  - Sarah Vaughan
- World musics
  - Africa and the Middle East
  - The Americas
  - Asia and the Pacific
  - Europe
- Basic stylistic characteristics representative of the region or nation
  - Musical style
  - Instrumentation

★ Given an excerpt of world music, can you identify its country or region of origin?

Music Theory

- Pitch concepts
  - Intervals

★ Given a printed representation of sheet music with two notes, can you identify the interval?

★ Given an excerpt of a melody being played, can you identify the intervals in the melody?

  - Chord
    - Major and minor triads
    - Major seventh
    - Dominant seventh
    - Diminished seventh
    - Half-diminished seventh
    - German augmented sixth
    - French augmented sixth
    - Italian augmented sixth

★ Given an excerpt of a chord being played, can you identify the chord quality?

★ Can you draw a music staff with the representation of a German augmented 6th chord?

★ Can you describe the function of a diminished 7th chord?

★ Given an excerpt of an augmented 6th chord being played in a progression, can you identify it?

★ Given a musical key, can you identify the parallel or relative major or minor, subdominant, and dominant keys?

► Scales and scale types

— Pentatonic

— Octatonic

— Whole-tone

— Chromatic

— Harmonic minor

— Melodic minor

— Major

► Modes

— Ionian

— Dorian

— Phrygian

— Lydian

— Mixolydian

— Aeolian

— Locrian

► Tonality

► Harmony

— Intervals

— Chords

— Arpeggios

— Major

— Minor

— Diminished

— Blues progression

★ Given an excerpt of a pentatonic scale being played, can you identify it?

★ Given a printed representation of music in the Lydian mode, can you identify it?

★ Given an excerpt of a melody in a minor key, can you identify it?

★ Can you draw a music staff with the representation of a diminished chord?

★ Given a printed representation of figured bass, can you add the harmonies that would realize it?

► Harmonic analysis and harmonic progression

★ Given an excerpt of a chord progression, can you draw a music staff that represents it?

★ Give an excerpt of a harmonic progression, can you identify what kind of cadence it ends with in relation to the opening tonic?

★ Given an excerpt with an example of a deceptive, authentic, plagal, or half cadence, can you identify it?

★ Given a printed representation of a melody, can you select the most appropriate chords to harmonize it?

★ Given a printed representation of music using common chord symbols from jazz and popular music, can you identify the chords?

- Rhythmic concepts, including meter and durational values
  - ▶ Accelerando
  - ▶ Anacrusis
  - ▶ Augmentation
  - ▶ Diminution
  - ▶ Hemiola
  - ▶ Hocket
  - ▶ Syncopation

★ Given a printed representation of an anacrusis, can you identify it?

★ Given a recorded musical excerpt, can you recognize the rhythm of the melody?

★ Given a printed musical excerpt, can you describe its metric organization?

★ Given a printed musical example with various metronome markings, can you describe the differences in tempo?

- Rhythmic notation
  - ▶ Beaming
  - ▶ Ties
  - ▶ Dotted notes
  - ▶ Double-dotted notes

★ Given a printed musical staff with a double-dotted note, can you describe the duration of that note?

- Musical form and analysis
  - ▶ Large-scale form
    - — Binary
    - — Theme and variations
    - — Fugue
  - ▶ Smaller formal structures
    - — Phrase structure
    - — Melodic motives
    - — Rhythmic motives

★ Given a recorded musical excerpt, can you identify from several printed excerpts the one that represents the main melodic phrase?

★ Given a recorded musical excerpt, can you describe the different cadences at the ends of the first and second phrases?

★ Given a recorded musical excerpt that uses the phrase structure ABACA, can you identify the phrase structure?

- Formal organization of musical excerpts
  - — Bar form
  - — Binary form
  - — Bridge
  - — Cadence
  - — Cadenza
  - — Coda
  - — Contrasting double period
  - — Development
  - — Episode
  - — Exposition
  - — Extension
  - — Fugue
  - — Melodic sequence
  - — Motive
  - — Parallel double period
  - — Phrase
  - — Recapitulation
  - — Rondo
  - — Sonata form
  - — Strophic form
  - — Subject
  - — Ternary form
  - — Theme and variations
  - — Through-composed

> ★ Given an excerpt consisting of the first two phrases of a composition for piano, can you identify how the two phrases are related?
>
> ★ Given a recorded musical excerpt, can you describe the order of the rhythmic transformations of the motive?
>
> ★ Can you describe the typical thematic development of sonata form in the eighteenth century?

- Musical texture
  - Monophony
  - Polyphony
  - Homophony
  - Heterophony

> ★ Given a printed musical excerpt, can you identify elements of imitation in the texture?
>
> ★ Given a recorded musical excerpt of a four-part ensemble, can you identify elements of the texture?

- Expressive elements
  - Dynamics
    - — Crescendo
    - — Descrescendo
    - — Marcato
    - — Ritardando
  - Articulation
    - — Accent
    - — Legato
    - — Rubato
    - — Staccato
  - Tempo
    - — Accelerando
    - — Adagio
    - — Andante
    - — Allegro
    - — Grave
    - — Largo
    - — Moderato
    - — Presto
    - — Rallentando
    - — Ritardando
    - — Ritenuto
    - — Subito meno mosso
    - — Subito più mosso
    - — Vivace
  - Timbre

> ★ Given a recorded musical excerpt that uses staccato, can you identify the type of articulation?
>
> ★ Given a recorded musical excerpt that uses accelerando, can you identify the change in tempo?
>
> ★ Can you explain what is meant by poco a poco?
>
> ★ Given a recorded musical excerpt that uses subito meno mosso, can you identify the change in tempo?

- Compositional devices
  - Augmentation
  - Basso ostinato
  - Bitonality
  - Diminution
  - Inversion
  - Metric modulation
  - Pedal point
  - Polymeters
  - Retrograde
  - Sequence
  - Serialism
  - Variation

★ Given a recorded musical excerpt that uses diminution, can you identify it?

★ Given a printed excerpt from J.S. Bach that uses a retrograde melody, can you identify this compositional device?

★ Given a recorded excerpt of a vocal duet, can you identify the relationship between the soprano and tenor parts?

Performance

- Musical instruments
  - Classification of instruments
    - — Aerophones
    - — Chordophones
    - — Idiophones
    - — Membranophones
  - Instrumentation of standard ensembles

★ Given a recorded musical excerpt with a bassoon solo, can you identify the solo instrument?

★ Given a recorded musical excerpt of an instrumental trio, can you identify the three instruments being played?

★ Given a musical score unmarked for instrumentation, can you identify the intended instrumentation from evidence such as clefs, key signatures, and range?

★ For a harmonic series based on a given fundamental tone, can you identify the succession of partials?

  - World and folk instruments (e.g., sitar, bagpipe, panpipes)

★ Given a recorded musical excerpt with a thumb piano, can you identify the instrument and classify it?

★ Given a recorded musical excerpt of a duet for acoustic guitar and harmonica, can you identify the instruments?

  - Electronic instruments (e.g., synthesizers and Theramin)

★ Can you describe appropriate technologies for creating a multimedia performance?

- Instrumental performance techniques
  - Flutter tongue
  - *Col legno*
  - Double stops
  - *Glissando*
  - Multiphonics
  - Mutes
  - *Pizzicato*
  - *Portamento*
  - Successive down bows

- Vocal types (e.g., soprano and tenor)
    - General vocal types (e.g., soprano, alto, tenor, baritone, and bass)
    - Specific characteristic types (e.g., coloratura soprano or mezzo soprano)

> ★ Given a recorded musical excerpt of a baritone singing, can you identify the vocal type?

- Vocal performance techniques
    - Falsetto
    - Sprechstimme
    - Sotto voce
- Music that combines instruments and voices

> ★ Given a recorded musical excerpt of the first movement of Mahler's Eight Symphony, can you identify the performing forces heard?

- Acoustics
    - Application to performance situations
    - Common acoustic problems of performance and rehearsal spaces

> ★ Given a diagram of a choral standing arrangement, could you discuss the acoustical implications?
>
> ★ What are the most important acoustic principles in seating arrangements for instrumental ensembles?

- Conducting skills and concepts
    - Conducting patterns for various meters and rhythms
    - Proper conducting of specific tempos and rhythmic contexts
        - — Accelerando
        - — Downbeats
        - — Ritardando
        - — Syncopation
        - — Upbeats

> ★ In a passage using syncopation, what would be the appropriate conducting technique?
>
> ★ What would be the appropriate conducting pattern for a passage in $\frac{7}{8}$ time?

- Score reading
    - Transposing instruments
    - Interpreting notation and symbols
    - Stylistic interpretation

> ★ Given a printed excerpt of music in the key of D major, can you transcribe it into the key of F major?
>
> ★ When an excerpt is transcribed from the key of F-sharp to the key of B, how does this impact the key signatures and accidentals?
>
> ★ What are the rules of transposition for the trumpet? the violin?

- Improvisation skills and concepts, and improvisational techniques, including jazz improvisation

> ★ How are progressions used in improvisation?
>
> ★ Give some example of ornamentations commonly used in jazz vocal improvisations.

- Analysis of errors in performance of recorded excerpts with reference to correctly printed scores
    - Intonation
    - Pitch
    - Rhythm
    - Tempo
    - Balance
    - Articulation
    - Dynamics and other expressive markings

> ★ Given a printed musical score and a recording of a performance based on it (which you listen to three times), can you identify the measure where an error in pitch occurs?
>
> ★ If you are told the error occurs in a specific measure, would you notice that the music is being played *forte* when it is notated to be played *piano?*

Music Learning, K–12

- Overall music program objectives as related to accepted standards
    - *The School Music Program: A New Vision*

> ★ According to *The School Music Program: A New Vision*, what are some appropriate musical achievements for students in grades K–4?
>
> ★ By approximately what grade level should students be able to play by ear simple melodies on a melodic instrument?
>
> ★ Describe appropriate course objectives for singing in general music classrooms at grades K–4, 5–8, and 9–12.

- Basic requirements of music programs for elementary, middle school/junior high school,
  and high school as related to accepted standards
    - *Opportunity-to-Learn Standards for Music Instruction: Grades PreK–12*
        - — Facilities
        - — Course offerings
        - — Scheduling
        - — Staffing
        - — Materials
        - — Equipment

> ★ Describe the music library and instrument storage facilities that are associated with a quality high school orchestra program.

- Effective and appropriate organization of curriculum according to generally recognized standards
    - Units
    - Lesson plans
    - Programs

> ★ Describe the course objectives that you might develop for a nine-week general music course that meets three times a week that is required for all eighth grade students in a district. Then write a lesson plan for one classroom period that would help to fulfill one of the course objectives.

- Scope as related to course content
  - Psychomotor, cognitive, and affective behaviors
  - Music concepts and elements

> ★ Describe how a teacher might include psychomotor, cognitive, and affective teaching and learning units when teaching beginning band students to play an arrangement of Beethoven's "Ode to Joy."
>
> ★ Give an example of an instructional activity that relates to what is called *Analysis* in Bloom's taxonomy of conceptual development.
>
> ★ Give an example of one that relates to *Comprehension*.

- Learning sequences
  - the transfer of learning approach
  - appropriate learning sequences for teaching various concepts

> ★ What is an appropriate learning sequence for teaching about rhythm? In what sequence should you introduce concepts such as subdivision in triple meter?
>
> ★ Describe an appropriate learning sequence for teaching the concept of harmony?

- Techniques for classroom and for rehearsal with choral or instrumental ensembles
  - Introducing concepts and skills

> ★ What is an effective strategy for introducing the concept of solfège to a class?

  - Teaching care of the instrument
    - — Bows
    - — Rosin
    - — Swabs
    - — Reeds
    - — Mouthpieces
    - — Assembly
  - Correcting specific problems
    - — Breath support
    - — Embouchure
    - — Soft palate
    - — Hand positions
    - — Stick grips
    - — Posture
    - — Fingerings

> ★ Describe three effective teaching techniques for correcting specific problems with woodwind embouchures, brass embouchures, stick grips, or bowing.

  - Overcoming technical challenges

> ★ What kinds of difficulties with rhythm would you expect from a seventh-grade orchestra?
>
> ★ What kinds of difficulties with harmony would you expect in a capella singing by an average high school chorus?
>
> ★ Given a score for a Sousa march, can you identify the aspects that are likely to be most challenging for a less advanced high school band?

- Appropriate repertoire
  - Standard repertoire for your specialty (e.g., general, band, chorus, or orchestra)
    - Elementary ensembles
    - Middle school ensembles
    - High school ensembles
  - Works that are appropriate for presenting basic music concepts in K–12 general music classes

★ Name four pieces that you would suggest including in a spring concert for a middle school ensemble (in your specialty)? Name three musical concepts you could teach from each work.

★ Name some arrangers who specialize in works that are appropriate for an elementary school ensemble (in your specialty).

★ What are some good musical excerpts to play to a general music class in elementary school to introduce the concept of syncopation?

★ What genre is usually associated with the work of Sammy Nestico?

- Methods of teaching singing in general music
  - Teaching rote songs
    - Why it's important
    - Teaching methods
  - Teaching sight-singing
    - Fixed do
    - Moveable do
    - Tonic sol-fa
    - Solfegietto

★ When is it more appropriate to use a whole-song rather than a phrase-by-phrase approach in teaching a song by rote?

★ Name some of the advantages and disadvantages of the fixed do method and the moveable methods of sight-singing.

- Basic principles and philosophies of pedagogical methods
  - Orff
  - Kodály
  - Dalcroze
  - Suzuki
  - Gordon

★ What are some musical activities associated with the Suzuki method?

★ Whose pedagogical method emphasizes presenting students with musical problems and expecting them to improvise independent solutions?

- Methods of evaluation and assessment
  - Musical aptitude tests
  - Strategies and resources for measuring students' musical development
  - Strategies and resources for providing feedback to enhance musical learning
  - Major research findings in music aptitude
- Music instruction for special and/or gifted students; accommodation strategies and guidelines appropriate in the music classroom or rehearsal setting
  - Students with special talents
  - Students with physical handicaps
  - Students with learning disabilities
  - Students with emotional disorders

★ What strategies would you use to help a student with dyslexia read sheet music?

- Music technology, equipment, and resources for the music classroom
  - Computers
  - MIDI
  - CD-ROM

★ Describe how you could use the Internet to teach a unit in [choose a topic] to students in K–4, grade 5–8, and grades 9–12.

★ Draw a diagram illustrating how you could set up a system for recording and playback that includes a CD player, CD recorder, and self-powered speakers. How might the setup differ if the speakers were not self-powered?

- Classroom management skills appropriate to the music classroom or ensemble rehearsal
  - Strategies for modeling and rewarding appropriate behaviors
  - Strategies for discouraging or correcting inappropriate behaviors

★ Describe two effective methods you have seen teachers use to control students' talking in class. Describe two *ineffective* methods you have seen teachers attempt to use.

Professional Practices

- Philosophies of music education
  - Leading figures and their viewpoints
  - Philosophies, ideas, and goals developed in national symposiums and conventions
    - — Contemporary Music Project
    - — Manhattanville Music Curriculum Project
    - — Yale Seminar on Music Education
    - — Tanglewood Symposium

★ How would you summarize the viewpoint of Bennett Reimer?

★ What aspects of educational philosophy contribute to Bruner's spiral curriculum?

★ Compare and contrast the value placed on music education by Plato and Aristotle. How does John Dewey's philosophy on the same topic compare?

- Music publications: journals, reference works, other source materials
  - *The New Handbook of Research on Music Teaching and Learning*
  - *National Standards for Arts Education*
  - *Journal of Research for Music Education*
  - *Bulletin for the Council of Research in Music Education*
  - *The School Music Program: A New Vision*
  - *Opportunity-to-Learn Standards for Music Instruction*
  - *Performance Standards for Music*

★ What source would be good for doing research about music history?

★ Name some standard reference works that should be in the collection of a high school library to help students complete projects in music history.

- Professional ethics
  - Copyright law
  - Appropriate business dealings with vendors and music merchants
  - Appropriate venus for performance by student ensembles

★ Is it ever appropriate to make duplicates of sheet music using a copy machine? If so, under what circumstances?

★ Would it be appropriate for a student ensemble to perform for a fee at a recreational festival that charges admission? Why or why not?

- Professional organizations, including their philosophies and goals
  - MENC: The National Association for Music Education
  - American Bandmasters Association
  - American Choral Directors Association
  - Americans for the Arts
  - American Orff-Schulwerk Association
  - Organization of American Kodaly Educators
  - American String Teachers Association with NSOA
  - American Society of Composers, Authors, and Publishers (ASCAP)
  - Music Publishers' Association
  - Music Teachers National Association
  - NAMM: The International Music Products Association
  - National Association of Schools of Music
  - National School Boards Association

★ What are some of the important publications of MENC in your specialty?

★ Which organization publishes Opportunity-to-Learn Standards for Music Instruction: Grades PreK–12?

★ What are some organizations of special interest to choral educators/string educators, band directors?

Chapter 4

Don't Be Defeated by Multiple-Choice Questions

► ► ► ► ► ► ► ► ► ► ► ►

Understanding Multiple-Choice Questions

When you read multiple-choice questions on the Praxis *Music: Content Knowledge* test, you will probably notice that the syntax (word order) is different from the word order you're used to seeing in ordinary material that you read, such as newspapers or textbooks. One of the reasons for this difference is that many test questions contain the phrase "which of the following."

In order to answer a multiple-choice question successfully, you need to consider carefully the context set up by the question and limit your choice of answers to the list given. The purpose of the phrase "which of the following" is to remind you to do this. For example, look at this question:

> Which of the following is a flavor made from beans?
>
> (A) Strawberry
> (B) Cherry
> (C) Vanilla
> (D) Mint

You may know that chocolate and coffee are also flavors made from beans, but they are not listed, and the question asks you to select from the list that follows ("which of the following"). So the answer has to be the only bean-derived flavor in the list: vanilla.

Notice that the answer can be substituted for the phrase "which of the following." In the question above, you could insert "vanilla" for "which of the following" and have the sentence "Vanilla is a flavor made from beans." Sometimes it helps to cross out "which of the following" and insert the various choices. You may want to give this technique a try as you answer various multiple-choice questions on the practice test.

Looking carefully at the "which of the following" phrase helps you to focus on what the question is asking you to find and on the answer choices. In the simple example above, all of the answer choices are flavors. Your job is to decide which of the flavors is the one made from beans.

The vanilla bean question is pretty straightforward. But the phrase "which of the following" can also be found in more challenging questions. Look at this question:

> Which of the following is an example of a critical thinking skill?
>
> (A) Students label the parts of a chord.
> (B) Students notate rhythmic patterns in all of the common meters.
> (C) Students compare two different recordings of the same work.
> (D) Students transpose a trumpet part from written pitch to concert pitch.

The placement of "which of the following" tells you that the list of choices is a list of examples (in this case, these are examples of things students might do). What are you supposed to find as an answer? You are supposed to find the choice that shows use of a critical-thinking skill.

Educational Testing Service (ETS) question-writers and editors work very hard to word each question as clearly as possible. Sometimes, though, it helps to put the question in your own words. Here, you could paraphrase the question as "Which of these student activities requires students to use critical thinking?" The correct answer is C. *When using this method, it is important* <u>*not to change the meaning*</u> *of the question by, for example, excluding important elements that set the context for you.*

You may also find that it helps you to circle or underline each of the critical details of the question in your test book so that you don't miss any of them. It's only by looking at all parts of the question carefully that you will have all of the information you need to answer it. Circle or underline the critical parts of what is being asked in this question.

Which of the following lists the musical genres in the correct chronological order of their development?

(A) Motet, string quartet, opera, symphonic poem
(B) Motet, opera, string quartet, symphonic poem
(C) Opera, motet, string quartet, symphonic poem
(D) Opera, symphonic poem, motet, string quartet

Here is one possible way you may have annotated the question:

Which of the following lists the musical genres in the correct chronological order of their development?

(A) Motet, string quartet, opera, symphonic poem
(B) Motet, opera, string quartet, symphonic poem
(C) Opera, motet, string quartet, symphonic poem
(D) Opera, symphonic poem, motet, string quartet

After thinking about the question, you can probably see that you are being asked to look at lists of musical genres and decide which one is ordered correctly by the eras in which the genres were developed. The correct answer is B. The important thing is understanding what the question is asking. With enough practice, you should be able to determine what any question is asking. Knowing the answer is, of course, a different matter, but you have to understand a question before you can answer it.

Understanding Questions Containing "NOT," "LEAST," or "EXCEPT"

The words "NOT," "EXCEPT," and "LEAST" can make comprehension of test questions more difficult. It asks you to select the choice that *doesn't* fit. You must be very careful with this question type, because it's easy to forget that you're selecting the negative. This question type is used in situations in which there are several good solutions, or ways to approach something, but also a clearly wrong way to do something. These words are always capitalized when they appear in The Praxis Series test questions, but they are easily (and frequently) overlooked.

For the following test question, determine what kind of answer you need and what the details of the question are.

> Under current United States copyright law, guidelines for educational uses ("fair use") of music permit all of the following EXCEPT
>
> (A) emergency copying to replace a purchase copy that is lost and is not available for an imminent performance
> (B) making a single copy of recordings of performances for evaluation or rehearsal purposes
> (C) making an arrangement of a copyrighted work for a school ensemble to perform
> (D) copying for the purpose of scholarly research

You're looking for a use of music that is NOT permitted for educational uses under United States copyright law. C is the correct answer—all of the other choices are permitted under current copyright law.

TIP

It's easy to get confused while you're processing the information to answer a question with a LEAST, NOT, or EXCEPT in the question. If you treat the word "LEAST," "NOT," or "EXCEPT" as one of the details you must satisfy, you have a better chance of understanding what the question is asking.

Be Familiar with Multiple-Choice Question Types

You will probably see more than one question format on a multiple-choice test. Here are examples of some of the more common question formats.

1. Complete the statement

In this type of question, you are given an incomplete statement. You must select the choice that will make the completed statement correct.

> Prior to learning about meter, elementary students should be able to demonstrate their understanding of
>
> (A) weak and strong beats
> (B) syncopation
> (C) subdivision of the beat
> (D) tempo markings

To check your answer, reread the question and add your answer choice at the end. Be sure that your choice best completes the sentence. The correct answer is A.

2. Questions about musical scores

The important thing to keep in mind when answering questions about musical scores is to answer the question that is asked. You should consider reading the questions first, and then looking at the musical score in light of the questions you have to answer.

Look at this example:

The excerpt above is taken from a lied in A minor by Alma Mahler. Which of the following best represents the bracketed harmony labeled X?

(A) ii^{7}
(B) $\text{vii}^{\circ 6}_{5}$
(C) Aug. 6
(D) V^{7}/V

The correct answer is D.

3. Questions based on listening examples

The questions will be spoken to you on the CD and also printed in the test book. Base your answer only on the particular excerpt that is played, unless the question specifically asks about the larger work from which the excerpt has been taken.

(Heard on tape: an excerpt from Ravel's "Laideronette, Impératrice des Pagodes" from Ma mère l'Oye)

What is the predominant scale or mode?

(A) Major
(B) Minor
(C) Pentatonic
(D) Chromatic

In the excerpt heard on the CD, the main melody is based on the pentatonic scale C#, D#, F#, G#, A#. The correct answer, therefore, is C.

4. Other formats

New question formats are developed from time to time in order to find new ways of assessing knowledge with multiple-choice questions. If you see a format with which you are not familiar, read the directions carefully. Then read and approach the question the way you would any other question, asking yourself what you are supposed to be looking for, and what details are given in the question that help you find the answer.

The Difference Between "Recall" Questions and "Best" Questions

Recall Questions

To function competently, musicians need to know certain technical facts off the top of their heads. They also need to be able to recall certain fundamentals, such as basic aspects of repertoire. The Praxis *Music: Content Knowledge* test includes some questions like this:

Which of the following operas was written by Benjamin Britten?

(A) *Boris Godunov*
(B) *Madame Butterfly*
(C) *Peter Grimes*
(D) *The Second Hurricane*

There is very little "reasoning-out" one can do with this question. One simply must have been exposed to enough basic repertoire to know that *Boris Godunov* is by Mussorgsky, *Madame Butterfly* is by Puccini, *Peter Grimes* is by Britten, and that *The Second Hurricane* is by Copland. The correct answer, therefore, is C. Choices A, B, and D are standard repertoire in international opera. Beware: Some test takers choose the piece they know, or the piece they think "ETS wants us to choose," and go on without giving the question any thought. Read the question and choose the answer you honestly think is right.

Ideas for study:

- What aspects of style would set these four composers apart?
- In what ways do their works exemplify national style characteristics?

Similarly, you are expected to be familiar enough with standard repertoire to recognize the style of prominent composers of any style or period. You may be played a recording of a work and then be asked to identify the composer, as in this example:

Who is the composer?

(A) Perotin
(B) Berlioz
(C) Debussy
(D) Messiaen

Although listening for style elements is more complicated than simply recalling names, the same basic principle applies: Your musical studies need to have covered enough basic, representative repertoire to either know the right answer or eliminate the wrong answers. Your music history courses and texts (e.g., Grout's *History of Western Music*) are a good place to begin, since these resources present important repertoire in historical, stylistic, and cultural contexts. The world around you offers many other opportunities for listening to and learning about all kinds of music.

Ideas for study:

- In your "mental CD player," can you "play" a selection that would represent the style of each one of these composers?
- What periods and styles do these composers represent?
- What makes these composers important, and where would you look to find out?

The composer question above could be asked in another way, as a historical period or chronology question. The answer would depend on the work heard on the CD.

What is the approximate date of composition?

(A) 1200
(B) 1830
(C) 1900
(D) 1960

Ideas for study:

- Using the rounded dates for each choice above (A through D), what four works might be heard on the test's CD?
- What genre does each work represent?

"Best" Questions

Many of the questions on the Praxis *Music: Content Knowledge* test will ask you to make contextual decisions—that is, ask you which option is "best," given the limits of the question and the context in which the topic is presented. As always, the words in the question are chosen specifically to help you get into the frame of mind that will give you the *best opportunity to choose the correct answer*. Here is an example:

Which of the following Roman numerals best describes the function of the first chord in the progression?

(A) ii
(B) iv
(C) V
(D) vii

Trained musicians know from their background in music theory that the best answer choice depends on the context in which the chord is found. You need to consider issues such as "What is the key signature?" and "What chords come after or around the one in question?" This chord . . .

. . . could be analyzed as ii in C major or iv in A minor. In this context . . .

. . . as the first chord in the progression, it is best analyzed as ii. Notice that the second chord is a V^6_5 of I in C major, and the third chord is, indeed, I—C major. In this context, the best choice would be A. In *this* context, however . . .

. . . it is best analyzed as iv in A minor, choice B. We see that the second chord is altered to raise the third, making it a V^4_3 of i in A minor.

Ideas for study:

- How would the printed examples differ if the right answer had been . . .
  - ❒ C?
  - ❒ D?
- What would the examples look like if they had been in . . .
  - ❒ E-flat major or C minor?
  - ❒ D major or B minor?

Questions on the *Music: Content Knowledge* test do not contain tricks; but while some are very easy, others may be more complex. You may recall that an important purpose of the test's questions is to make sure the test takers *know and understand* the training music teachers are expected to have. Understanding how chords function in tonal progressions and understanding enough to identify those functions in context are basic to training about theory. Since music educators work with real music virtually every day, you are likely to encounter questions on this test that are based on printed excerpts from *real pieces of music*, with all the transpositions and other distractions that you would find in a real piece of music.

Ideas for study:

- Pick a score off the shelf in your library's music collection, open the score to any random page, and analyze a chord progression in one of the measures on that page.
- Get out your old music theory texts and review the advanced or difficult chord types, especially those you found hard to deal with during your coursework (e.g. augmented sixth chords, diminished seventh chords, and so on).

As you will see from the sample test questions on the enclosed CD and the explanations in chapter 6, you may also be expected to show evidence that you can identify chords, chord progressions, rhythmic motives, meter signatures, scales and modes, and expressive elements by ear.

Ideas for study:

- Organize a study group. Each of you can play a short, simple chord progression while the others transcribe it.
- In the same kind of group, have everyone write out short chord progressions. Swap them so that everyone can practice identifying chord functions (e.g., subdominant, dominant, etc.) and modulation goals (e.g., ends in relative minor, parallel major, Picardy third, and so on).

Other Useful Facts about the Test

1. **In the second part of the test (the part *not* paced by the tape being played), you can answer the questions in any order.** You can go through the questions from beginning to end, as many test takers do, or you can create your own path. Perhaps you will want to answer questions in your strongest area of knowledge first and then move from your strengths to your weaker areas. There is no right or wrong way. Use the approach that works best for you.

2. **There are no trick questions on the test.** You don't have to find any hidden meanings or worry about trick wording. All of the questions on the test ask about subject matter knowledge in a straightforward manner.

3. **Don't worry about answer patterns.** There is one myth that says that answers on multiple-choice tests follow patterns. There is another myth that there will never be more than two questions with the same lettered answer following each other. There is no truth to either of these myths. Select the answer you think is correct, based on your knowledge of the subject.

4. **There is no penalty for guessing.** The multiple-choice part of your test score is based on the number of correct answers you have. When you don't know the answer to a question, try to eliminate any obviously wrong answers and then guess at the correct one.

5. **It's OK to write in your test booklet.** You can work out problems right on the pages of the booklet, make notes to yourself, mark questions you want to review later, or write anything at all. Your test booklet will be destroyed after you are finished with it, so use it in any way that is helpful to you. But make sure to mark your answers on the answer sheet.

Smart Tips for Taking the Test

1. **Put your answers in the right "bubbles."** It seems obvious, but be sure that you are filling in the answer "bubble" that corresponds to the question you are answering. A significant number of test takers fill in a bubble without checking to see that the number matches the question they are answering.

2. **Skip the questions you find extremely difficult.** There are sure to be some questions that you think are hard. If you are, for example, a general music specialist, a question about advanced high school band or choral repertoire may lie outside your area of expertise. Rather than trying to answer these on your first pass through the test, leave them blank and mark them in your test booklet so that you can come back to them later.

   Pay attention to the time as you answer the rest of the questions on the test, and try to finish with 10 or 15 minutes remaining so that you can go back over the questions you left blank. Even if you don't know the answer the second time you read the questions, see if you can narrow down the possible answers, and then guess.

Since the Praxis *Music* examinations are used by states to certify K-12 music educators of all specialties, you may find questions on the *Music: Content Knowledge* test pertaining to issues that were not central to your particular specialty. States take this aspect of the tests into account when they set passing scores, so you do not need to answer every question correctly to pass the test. Do not worry about these questions. When you encounter such a question, simply choose what you think is the best answer and move on, or mark the question in your test book and return to it after you have answered questions with which you are more familiar.

3. **Keep track of the time.** Bring a watch to the test, just in case the clock in the test room is difficult for you to see. You will probably have plenty of time to answer all of the questions, but if you find yourself becoming bogged down in one section, you might decide to move on and come back to that section later.

4. **Read all of the possible answers before selecting one**—and then reread the question to be sure the answer you have selected really answers the question being asked. Remember that a question that contains a phrase such as "Which of the following does NOT . . ." is asking for the one answer that is NOT a correct statement or conclusion.

5. **Check your answers.** If you have extra time left over at the end of the test, look over each question and make sure that you have filled in the "bubble" on the answer sheet as you intended. Many test takers make careless mistakes that they could have corrected if they had checked their answers.

6. **Don't worry about your score when you are taking the test.** No one is expected to answer all of the questions correctly. Your score on this test is not analogous to your score on the SAT, the GRE, or other similar-looking (but in fact very different!) tests. It doesn't matter on this test whether you score very high or barely pass. If you meet the minimum passing scores for your state, and you meet the state's other requirements for obtaining a teaching license, you will receive a license. In other words, your actual score doesn't matter, as long as it is above the minimum required score. With your score report you will receive a booklet entitled *Understanding Your Praxis Scores*, which lists the passing scores for your state.

7. **Use your energy to take the test, not to get angry at it.** Getting angry at the test only elevates test anxiety, decreasing the likelihood that you will do your best on the test. Highly qualified music educators and test development professionals (all with backgrounds in teaching music) worked diligently to make the test the best it could be. Your state had the test painstakingly reviewed before adopting it as a licensure requirement. The best thing to do is concentrate on answering the questions as well as you can. Take the test, do your best, pass it, and get on with your career.

Chapter 5

Practice Test, *Music: Content Knowledge*

► ► ► ► ► ► ► ► ► ► ► ►

CHAPTER 5

Now that you have studied the content topics and have worked through strategies for answering multiple-choice questions, you should take the following practice test. You will need to use a CD player for the first section, Questions 1–27. Index numbers 1–27 on the enclosed CD include all of the recorded excerpts for the first section of the test (see appendix C for a list of the CD's contents, but wait until after you take the practice test before you do this). You may find it helpful to simulate actual testing conditions, giving yourself about 90 minutes to work on the questions. You can cut out and use the answer sheet provided if you wish.

Keep in mind that the test you take at an actual administration will have different questions, although the proportion of questions in each area and major subarea will be approximately the same. You should not expect the percentage of questions you answer correctly in this practice test to be exactly the same as when you take the test at an actual administration, since numerous factors affect a person's performance in any given testing situation.

When you have finished the practice questions, you can score your answers and read the explanations of the best answer choices in chapter 6.

THE **PRAXIS**
S E R I E S
Professional Assessments for Beginning Teachers®

TEST NAME:

Music: Content Knowledge

Practice Questions

Time—approximately 90 Minutes
90 Questions

(Note: At the official test administration, there will be 135 questions, and you will be allowed approximately 120 minutes to complete the test.)

DO NOT USE INK

Use only a pencil with soft black lead (No. 2 or HB) to complete this answer sheet.
Be sure to fill in completely the oval that corresponds to the proper letter or number.
Completely erase any errors or stray marks.

THE PRAXIS SERIES
Professional Assessments for Beginning Teachers®

Answer Sheet C

PAGE 1

1. NAME
Enter your last name and first initial.
Omit spaces, hyphens, apostrophes, etc.

Last Name (first 6 letters) | F I

A B C D E F G H I J K L M N O P Q R S T U V W X Y Z

2.

YOUR NAME: (Print) ______________________
Last Name (Family or Surname) First Name (Given) M. I.

MAILING ADDRESS: (Print) ______________________
P.O. Box or Street Address Apt. # (If any)

____
City State or Province

____
Country Zip or Postal Code

TELEPHONE NUMBER: ( ) ______ ( ) ______
Home Business

SIGNATURE: ______________ TEST DATE: ______________

3. DATE OF BIRTH

Month: Jan. Feb. Mar. April May June July Aug. Sept. Oct. Nov. Dec.

Day: 0 1 2 3 | 0 1 2 3 4 5 6 7 8 9

4. SOCIAL SECURITY NUMBER

0 1 2 3 4 5 6 7 8 9

5. CANDIDATE ID NUMBER

0 1 2 3 4 5 6 7 8 9

6. TEST CENTER / REPORTING LOCATION

Center Number ______ Room Number ______

Center Name ______

City ______ State or Province ______

Country ______

7. TEST CODE / FORM CODE

0 1 2 3 4 5 6 7 8 9

8. TEST BOOK SERIAL NUMBER

9. TEST FORM

10. TEST NAME

51055 • 08920 • TF71M500
MH01159 Q2573-06

I.N. 202974

1 2 3 4

CERTIFICATION STATEMENT: (Please write the following statement below. DO NOT PRINT.)

"I hereby agree to the conditions set forth in the *Registration Bulletin* and certify that I am the person whose name and address appear on this answer sheet."

____

____

____

SIGNATURE: ________________________ **DATE:** _____ / _____ / _____

Month Day Year

BE SURE EACH MARK IS DARK AND COMPLETELY FILLS THE INTENDED SPACE AS ILLUSTRATED HERE: ● .

1 Ⓐ Ⓑ Ⓒ Ⓓ	41 Ⓐ Ⓑ Ⓒ Ⓓ	81 Ⓐ Ⓑ Ⓒ Ⓓ	121 Ⓐ Ⓑ Ⓒ Ⓓ
2 Ⓐ Ⓑ Ⓒ Ⓓ	42 Ⓐ Ⓑ Ⓒ Ⓓ	82 Ⓐ Ⓑ Ⓒ Ⓓ	122 Ⓐ Ⓑ Ⓒ Ⓓ
3 Ⓐ Ⓑ Ⓒ Ⓓ	43 Ⓐ Ⓑ Ⓒ Ⓓ	83 Ⓐ Ⓑ Ⓒ Ⓓ	123 Ⓐ Ⓑ Ⓒ Ⓓ
4 Ⓐ Ⓑ Ⓒ Ⓓ	44 Ⓐ Ⓑ Ⓒ Ⓓ	84 Ⓐ Ⓑ Ⓒ Ⓓ	124 Ⓐ Ⓑ Ⓒ Ⓓ
5 Ⓐ Ⓑ Ⓒ Ⓓ	45 Ⓐ Ⓑ Ⓒ Ⓓ	85 Ⓐ Ⓑ Ⓒ Ⓓ	125 Ⓐ Ⓑ Ⓒ Ⓓ
6 Ⓐ Ⓑ Ⓒ Ⓓ	46 Ⓐ Ⓑ Ⓒ Ⓓ	86 Ⓐ Ⓑ Ⓒ Ⓓ	126 Ⓐ Ⓑ Ⓒ Ⓓ
7 Ⓐ Ⓑ Ⓒ Ⓓ	47 Ⓐ Ⓑ Ⓒ Ⓓ	87 Ⓐ Ⓑ Ⓒ Ⓓ	127 Ⓐ Ⓑ Ⓒ Ⓓ
8 Ⓐ Ⓑ Ⓒ Ⓓ	48 Ⓐ Ⓑ Ⓒ Ⓓ	88 Ⓐ Ⓑ Ⓒ Ⓓ	128 Ⓐ Ⓑ Ⓒ Ⓓ
9 Ⓐ Ⓑ Ⓒ Ⓓ	49 Ⓐ Ⓑ Ⓒ Ⓓ	89 Ⓐ Ⓑ Ⓒ Ⓓ	129 Ⓐ Ⓑ Ⓒ Ⓓ
10 Ⓐ Ⓑ Ⓒ Ⓓ	50 Ⓐ Ⓑ Ⓒ Ⓓ	90 Ⓐ Ⓑ Ⓒ Ⓓ	130 Ⓐ Ⓑ Ⓒ Ⓓ
11 Ⓐ Ⓑ Ⓒ Ⓓ	51 Ⓐ Ⓑ Ⓒ Ⓓ	91 Ⓐ Ⓑ Ⓒ Ⓓ	131 Ⓐ Ⓑ Ⓒ Ⓓ
12 Ⓐ Ⓑ Ⓒ Ⓓ	52 Ⓐ Ⓑ Ⓒ Ⓓ	92 Ⓐ Ⓑ Ⓒ Ⓓ	132 Ⓐ Ⓑ Ⓒ Ⓓ
13 Ⓐ Ⓑ Ⓒ Ⓓ	53 Ⓐ Ⓑ Ⓒ Ⓓ	93 Ⓐ Ⓑ Ⓒ Ⓓ	133 Ⓐ Ⓑ Ⓒ Ⓓ
14 Ⓐ Ⓑ Ⓒ Ⓓ	54 Ⓐ Ⓑ Ⓒ Ⓓ	94 Ⓐ Ⓑ Ⓒ Ⓓ	134 Ⓐ Ⓑ Ⓒ Ⓓ
15 Ⓐ Ⓑ Ⓒ Ⓓ	55 Ⓐ Ⓑ Ⓒ Ⓓ	95 Ⓐ Ⓑ Ⓒ Ⓓ	135 Ⓐ Ⓑ Ⓒ Ⓓ
16 Ⓐ Ⓑ Ⓒ Ⓓ	56 Ⓐ Ⓑ Ⓒ Ⓓ	96 Ⓐ Ⓑ Ⓒ Ⓓ	136 Ⓐ Ⓑ Ⓒ Ⓓ
17 Ⓐ Ⓑ Ⓒ Ⓓ	57 Ⓐ Ⓑ Ⓒ Ⓓ	97 Ⓐ Ⓑ Ⓒ Ⓓ	137 Ⓐ Ⓑ Ⓒ Ⓓ
18 Ⓐ Ⓑ Ⓒ Ⓓ	58 Ⓐ Ⓑ Ⓒ Ⓓ	98 Ⓐ Ⓑ Ⓒ Ⓓ	138 Ⓐ Ⓑ Ⓒ Ⓓ
19 Ⓐ Ⓑ Ⓒ Ⓓ	59 Ⓐ Ⓑ Ⓒ Ⓓ	99 Ⓐ Ⓑ Ⓒ Ⓓ	139 Ⓐ Ⓑ Ⓒ Ⓓ
20 Ⓐ Ⓑ Ⓒ Ⓓ	60 Ⓐ Ⓑ Ⓒ Ⓓ	100 Ⓐ Ⓑ Ⓒ Ⓓ	140 Ⓐ Ⓑ Ⓒ Ⓓ
21 Ⓐ Ⓑ Ⓒ Ⓓ	61 Ⓐ Ⓑ Ⓒ Ⓓ	101 Ⓐ Ⓑ Ⓒ Ⓓ	141 Ⓐ Ⓑ Ⓒ Ⓓ
22 Ⓐ Ⓑ Ⓒ Ⓓ	62 Ⓐ Ⓑ Ⓒ Ⓓ	102 Ⓐ Ⓑ Ⓒ Ⓓ	142 Ⓐ Ⓑ Ⓒ Ⓓ
23 Ⓐ Ⓑ Ⓒ Ⓓ	63 Ⓐ Ⓑ Ⓒ Ⓓ	103 Ⓐ Ⓑ Ⓒ Ⓓ	143 Ⓐ Ⓑ Ⓒ Ⓓ
24 Ⓐ Ⓑ Ⓒ Ⓓ	64 Ⓐ Ⓑ Ⓒ Ⓓ	104 Ⓐ Ⓑ Ⓒ Ⓓ	144 Ⓐ Ⓑ Ⓒ Ⓓ
25 Ⓐ Ⓑ Ⓒ Ⓓ	65 Ⓐ Ⓑ Ⓒ Ⓓ	105 Ⓐ Ⓑ Ⓒ Ⓓ	145 Ⓐ Ⓑ Ⓒ Ⓓ
26 Ⓐ Ⓑ Ⓒ Ⓓ	66 Ⓐ Ⓑ Ⓒ Ⓓ	106 Ⓐ Ⓑ Ⓒ Ⓓ	146 Ⓐ Ⓑ Ⓒ Ⓓ
27 Ⓐ Ⓑ Ⓒ Ⓓ	67 Ⓐ Ⓑ Ⓒ Ⓓ	107 Ⓐ Ⓑ Ⓒ Ⓓ	147 Ⓐ Ⓑ Ⓒ Ⓓ
28 Ⓐ Ⓑ Ⓒ Ⓓ	68 Ⓐ Ⓑ Ⓒ Ⓓ	108 Ⓐ Ⓑ Ⓒ Ⓓ	148 Ⓐ Ⓑ Ⓒ Ⓓ
29 Ⓐ Ⓑ Ⓒ Ⓓ	69 Ⓐ Ⓑ Ⓒ Ⓓ	109 Ⓐ Ⓑ Ⓒ Ⓓ	149 Ⓐ Ⓑ Ⓒ Ⓓ
30 Ⓐ Ⓑ Ⓒ Ⓓ	70 Ⓐ Ⓑ Ⓒ Ⓓ	110 Ⓐ Ⓑ Ⓒ Ⓓ	150 Ⓐ Ⓑ Ⓒ Ⓓ
31 Ⓐ Ⓑ Ⓒ Ⓓ	71 Ⓐ Ⓑ Ⓒ Ⓓ	111 Ⓐ Ⓑ Ⓒ Ⓓ	151 Ⓐ Ⓑ Ⓒ Ⓓ
32 Ⓐ Ⓑ Ⓒ Ⓓ	72 Ⓐ Ⓑ Ⓒ Ⓓ	112 Ⓐ Ⓑ Ⓒ Ⓓ	152 Ⓐ Ⓑ Ⓒ Ⓓ
33 Ⓐ Ⓑ Ⓒ Ⓓ	73 Ⓐ Ⓑ Ⓒ Ⓓ	113 Ⓐ Ⓑ Ⓒ Ⓓ	153 Ⓐ Ⓑ Ⓒ Ⓓ
34 Ⓐ Ⓑ Ⓒ Ⓓ	74 Ⓐ Ⓑ Ⓒ Ⓓ	114 Ⓐ Ⓑ Ⓒ Ⓓ	154 Ⓐ Ⓑ Ⓒ Ⓓ
35 Ⓐ Ⓑ Ⓒ Ⓓ	75 Ⓐ Ⓑ Ⓒ Ⓓ	115 Ⓐ Ⓑ Ⓒ Ⓓ	155 Ⓐ Ⓑ Ⓒ Ⓓ
36 Ⓐ Ⓑ Ⓒ Ⓓ	76 Ⓐ Ⓑ Ⓒ Ⓓ	116 Ⓐ Ⓑ Ⓒ Ⓓ	156 Ⓐ Ⓑ Ⓒ Ⓓ
37 Ⓐ Ⓑ Ⓒ Ⓓ	77 Ⓐ Ⓑ Ⓒ Ⓓ	117 Ⓐ Ⓑ Ⓒ Ⓓ	157 Ⓐ Ⓑ Ⓒ Ⓓ
38 Ⓐ Ⓑ Ⓒ Ⓓ	78 Ⓐ Ⓑ Ⓒ Ⓓ	118 Ⓐ Ⓑ Ⓒ Ⓓ	158 Ⓐ Ⓑ Ⓒ Ⓓ
39 Ⓐ Ⓑ Ⓒ Ⓓ	79 Ⓐ Ⓑ Ⓒ Ⓓ	119 Ⓐ Ⓑ Ⓒ Ⓓ	159 Ⓐ Ⓑ Ⓒ Ⓓ
40 Ⓐ Ⓑ Ⓒ Ⓓ	80 Ⓐ Ⓑ Ⓒ Ⓓ	120 Ⓐ Ⓑ Ⓒ Ⓓ	160 Ⓐ Ⓑ Ⓒ Ⓓ

FOR ETS USE ONLY	R1	R2	R3	R4	R5	R6	R7	R8	TR	CS

SECTION I
Time—approximately 30 minutes
27 Questions

Directions: In this section of the test, you will be asked questions about recorded musical excerpts that will be played for you. Each question will be read aloud on the recording, except when two or more questions are related to the same musical excerpt, in which case you will be given time to read the questions to yourself. Each question, followed by four possible answers, is also printed in the test book. After listening to the excerpt, choose the best answer in each case and then fill in the corresponding lettered space on the answer sheet with a heavy, dark mark so that you cannot see the letter. Listen to the following sample question and recorded excerpt, and choose the best answer.

Sample Question: Who is the composer?

(A) Brahms
(B) Beethoven
(C) Mozart
(D) Bach

SAMPLE ANSWER

Since the question asks you to identify the composer of the recorded excerpt, and the composer is Beethoven, you would mark response (B) on your answer sheet.

For each question, base your answer only on the particular excerpt you hear, unless the question specifically asks about the larger work from which the excerpt has been taken. Each excerpt will be played once, unless otherwise indicated.

1. What is the texture?

(A) Imitative polyphony
(B) Nonimitative polyphony
(C) Monophony
(D) Homophony

2. What is the style or period?

(A) Baroque
(B) Classical
(C) Romantic
(D) Impressionist

3. What is the country or region of origin?

(A) Appalachia
(B) India
(C) Japan
(D) South America

4. What is the genre?

(A) Fugue
(B) Passacaglia
(C) Chorale prelude
(D) Toccata

Questions 5–6 are based on a single excerpt.The excerpt will be played two times. Before listening to the excerpt for the first time, please read **Questions 5–6.**

Now listen to the excerpt and begin to answer **Questions 5-6.**

5. In relation to the opening tonic, the excerpt ends in which of the following keys?

   (A) Tonic
   (B) Dominant
   (C) Relative minor
   (D) Subdominant

Now listen to the excerpt again and finish answering **Questions 5–6.**

6. Who is the composer?

   (A) Mozart
   (B) Bartók
   (C) Chopin
   (D) Brahms

Questions 7–8 are based on a single excerpt. The excerpt will be played two times. Before listening to the excerpt for the first time, please read **Questions 7–8.**

Now listen to the excerpt and begin to answer **Questions 7–8.**

7. What musical device is heard at the beginning of the excerpt?

   (A) Ritardando
   (B) Accelerando
   (C) Subito meno mosso
   (D) Subito più mosso

Now listen to the excerpt again and finish answering **Questions 7–8.**

8. Who is the composer?

   (A) Aaron Copland
   (B) Howard Hanson
   (C) Libby Larsen
   (D) Ellen Taaffe Zwilich

Questions 9–10 are based on a single excerpt. The excerpt will be played two times. Before listening to the excerpt for the first time, please read **Questions 9–10.**

Now listen to the excerpt and begin to answer **Questions 9–10.**

9. Which of the following best describes the texture of the excerpt?

   (A) Soprano solo, accompanied by a drone
   (B) Soprano solo, accompanied by a basso continuo
   (C) Soprano solo alternating with chorus, both accompanied by a drone
   (D) Soprano solo alternating with chorus, both accompanied by a ground bass

Now listen to the excerpt again and finish answering Questions 9–10.

10. What is the approximate date of composition?

   (A) 1150
   (B) 1430
   (C) 1600
   (D) 1730

11. Who is the jazz soloist?

    (A) Louis Armstrong
    (B) Wynton Marsalis
    (C) Charlie Parker
    (D) Benny Goodman

12. What is the interval? (The interval will be played <u>two</u> times.)

    (A) Minor third
    (B) Major third
    (C) Perfect fourth
    (D) Perfect fifth

13. The first phrase of the melody played by the brass is given below.

Which of the following correctly notates the second phrase? (The excerpt will be played three times.)

(A) 

(B) 

(C) 

(D) 

---

14. What is the form of the excerpt? (The excerpt will be played <u>two</u> times.)

    (A) Contrasting double period, with extension of the last phrase
    (B) Contrasting double period, without extension of the last phrase
    (C) Parallel double period, with extension of the last phrase
    (D) Parallel double period, without extension of the last phrase

15. Which of the following diagrams best represents the phrase structure of the excerpt? (The excerpt will be played two times.)

    (A) a a
    (B) a b c
    (C) a a' a'' a'''
    (D) a a' b b'

16. Which of the following would be the most appropriate conducting pattern? (The excerpt will be played two times.)
    (A) A 2-beat pattern, using one short beat and one long beat (2 + 3)
    (B) A 2-beat pattern, using one long beat and one short beat (3 + 2)
    (C) A 3-beat pattern, using two short beats and one long beat (2 + 2 + 3)
    (D) A 3-beat pattern, using one long beat and two short beats (3 + 2 + 2)

17. The excerpt is part of a traditional musical culture of which of the following regions?
    (A) Middle East
    (B) North America
    (C) Australia
    (D) Caribbean

18. What is the country of origin?
    (A) Cuba
    (B) France
    (C) Jamaica
    (D) Italy

19. What is the chord quality? (The chord will be played two times.)
    (A) Diminished
    (B) Minor
    (C) Major
    (D) Augmented

Questions 20–21 are based on a single excerpt. The excerpt will be played two times. Before listening to the excerpt for the first time, please read **Questions 20–21.**

Now listen to the excerpt and begin to answer **Questions 20–21.**

20. The excerpt consists of the first two phrases of a composition for piano. How are the two phrases related?
    (A) The second phrase is an exact repetition of the first phrase.
    (B) The second phrase is a varied repetition of the first phrase.
    (C) The second phrase is a transposition of the first phrase.
    (D) The second phrase provides material that contrasts with the first phrase.

Now listen to the excerpt again and finish answering **Questions 20–21.**

21. The style of the excerpt indicates that it was composed during which of the following time periods?
    (A) 1685-1750
    (B) 1750-1820
    (C) 1820-1880
    (D) 1880-1940

22. What is the predominant rhythmic device?

    (A) Syncopation
    (B) Hemiola
    (C) Rubato
    (D) Anacrusis

23. Which of the following correctly identifies the style and the approximate time period in which the recording was made?

    (A) Dixieland . . 1920's
    (B) Swing . . 1930's
    (C) Rock 'n' roll . . 1950's
    (D) Free jazz . . 1960's

24. Which of the following correctly notates the descending arpeggio? (The arpeggio will be played two times.)

25. Which of the following is heard in the snare drum?

    (A) Rim shot
    (B) Flam
    (C) Drag
    (D) Paradiddle

Directions: For Questions 26–27, you will hear excerpts of performances based on correct musical scores that appear in your test book. Each excerpt contains a single performance error. As each excerpt is played, find the measure or part of the measure in which the performance error occurs, and select the corresponding answer.

26. There are no pitch errors in the excerpt. Which measure contains a performance error? (The excerpt will be played three times.)

    (A) Measure 1
    (B) Measure 2
    (C) Measure 3
    (D) Measure 4

27. Which of the following errors is heard in the performance? (The excerpt will be played three times.)

(A) The chorus fails to observe the decrescendo.
(B) The chorus exaggerates the decrescendo.
(C) The chorus fails to begin the first note together.
(D) The chorus fails to end the last note together.

STOP

This is the end of the recorded section of the practice test.

Go on to the next section of the Content Knowledge practice test.

SECTION II
Time—60 minutes
63 Questions

Directions: Each of the questions or incomplete statements below is followed by four suggested answers or completions. Select the one that is best in each case and then fill in the corresponding lettered space on the answer sheet with a heavy, dark mark so that you cannot see the letter.

BASIC MUSICIANSHIP

28. A transposed band score shows the alto saxophone part written in the key of D major. In what key are the parts for horns in F written?

    (A) C
    (B) B♭
    (C) F
    (D) E

29. In a jazz piece that depends heavily on improvisation, which of the following elements is most likely to remain constant throughout the piece?

    (A) The number of performers playing at any given time
    (B) The ornamentation of the main melody
    (C) The harmonic pattern that forms the basis of the accompaniment
    (D) The tessitura of the solo instrument in each successive section

Questions 30–31 are based on the excerpt below.

30. What is the lowest note sung by the tenor?

 (A) F#
 (B) G#
 (C) A#
 (D D#

31. Which of the following notates the English horn part in concert pitch?

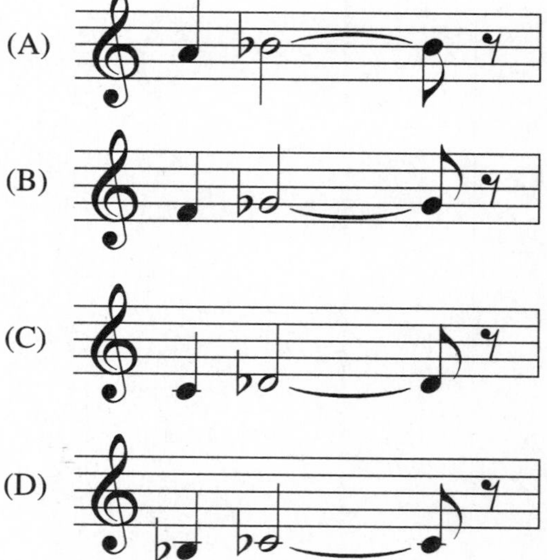

32. Which of the following conducting pattern sequences would be most appropriate for conducting the four measures above?

(A) $\frac{3}{4} + \frac{6}{4}$ (3 + 3) + $\frac{3}{4} + \frac{4}{4}$

(B) $\frac{3}{4}$ (in one) + $\frac{5}{4}$ (2 + 3) + $\frac{3}{4} + \frac{4}{4}$

(C) $\frac{3}{4} + \frac{5}{4}$ (3 + 2) + $\frac{3}{4} + \frac{4}{4}$

(D) $\frac{3}{4} + \frac{5}{4}$ (2 + 3) + $\frac{3}{4} + \frac{4}{4}$

33. Measures written in $\frac{5}{8}$ meter may be conducted in five beats per measure or in two beats per measure, depending on the

(A) tempo of the music
(B) dynamics in the music
(C) date of composition
(D) form of the music

34. Which of the following notates the next two partials for the harmonic series based on the fundamental tone given above?

---

35. During the eighteenth and nineteenth centuries, which of the following typically involved improvisation as part of the performance?

(A) Ritornello
(B) Divertimento
(C) Cadenza
(D) Fugue

Questions 36–37 refer to the excerpt on this page.

36. The performing ensemble indicated in the score consists of

(A) Baroque orchestra and horn quartet
(B) Baroque orchestra and vocal quartet
(C) Classical orchestra and three-part chorus
(D) Classical orchestra and four-part chorus

37. In bars 78–81, what bowing technique is specified in the first violin part?

(A) Martelé
(B) Détaché
(C) Ricochet
(D) Louré

38. What is the relationship between the duration of the half notes in measure 2 and those in measure 3 ?

(A) The duration of the half notes is the same in both measures.
(B) The duration of the half notes is shorter in measure 3 than in measure 2.
(C) The duration of the half notes is longer in measure 3 than in measure 2.
(D) The relative duration of the half notes in measures 2 and 3 is left to the discretion of the performer.

Question 39 is based on the excerpt below.

39. The excerpt is scored for which of the following performing ensembles?

    (A) Brass quartet
    (B) String quartet
    (C) Woodwind quartet
    (D) Two violins and basso continuo (cello and harpsichord)

---

40. Which of the following statements is true of the preparatory beat in conducting?

    (A) It should be rhythmically exaggerated.
    (B) It should be subdivided.
    (C) It indicates the opening tempo and dynamic.
    (D) It is always the gesture for beat 1 of the conducting pattern used.

MUSIC LEARNING, K–12

41. A teacher seeking consensus-based recommendations concerning what students should know and be able to do in music in grades 4, 8, and 12 would do best to consult which of these publications?

    (A) *Handbook of Research on Music Teaching and Learning*
    (B) *National Standards for Arts Education*
    (C) *Opportunity-to-Learn Standards for Arts Education*
    (D) *Strategies for Teaching: Guide for Music Methods Classes*

42. Which of the following course offerings best reflects Reimer's philosophy of aesthetic education?

    (A) Private instrumental or vocal instruction for any interested student
    (B) General music courses that involve listening, composing, and performing for all students
    (C) Performance-driven courses that prepare students for giving instrumental and vocal concerts
    (D) General music courses that focus on training students in aural and performance skills

43. Which of the following is most important in Zoltán Kodály's method of elementary music education?

    (A) Recorders
    (B) Xylophones
    (C) Unpitched percussion
    (D) Voices

44. Which of the following is best described as an affective student response to a performance of a jazz piece?

    (A) The student identifies the mode of the piece.
    (B) The student analyzes the form of the piece.
    (C) The student recognizes the performer.
    (D) The student asks to hear the piece again.

45. Which of the following composers is the best source of madrigals for performance by a high school choir?

    (A) Morley
    (B) Handel
    (C) Palestrina
    (D) Byrd

46. Which of the following is true about CD-ROM multimedia software in music instruction?

    (A) It works best with high school and college students.
    (B) It encourages interactive learning.
    (C) It requires a MIDI keyboard.
    (D) It is distributed most often on floppy disk.

47. Which of the following represents the most appropriate sequence of discrimination tasks for developing a child's sense of pitch?

    (A) High and low pitches; direction of melodic movement; movement by step and by skip
    (B) Movement by step and by skip; high and low pitches; direction of melodic movement
    (C) Direction of melodic movement; high and low pitches; movement by step and by skip
    (D) Direction of melodic movement; movement by step and by skip; high and low pitches

Praxis Pretest

28. D (A) Transposing 29. C 30. A. 31. A. (C) 32. C 33. A. 34. A. (C) Harmonics

35. C. 36. B. (D) orchestra 37. D. (A) Bowing 38. B. 39. B. 40. C 41.

41. A. (B) NATS 42. C (B) 43. A (D) 44. C (D) 45. C (A) 46. B 47. A.

48. B (C.) 49. C (A) 50. C (A) 51. C 52. C 53. A 54. C

55. B 56. A 57. D (B) 58. A 59. C 60. C 61. C (D)

62. B (D) 63. D (C.) 64. A (D) 65. A 66. D (A) 67. A (B) 68. C.

69. C 70. C 71. B 72. C 73. D. 74. A. 75. B

76. C (D) 77. A. 78. A (D) 79. D (B) 80. A 81. A

82. B 83. A 84. B. 85. C. (B) 86. B. 87. C.

88. C. 89. C. (D) 90. B.

- Transposing
- Harmonics
- Orchestra Instrumentation
- Bowing Techniques
- National standards for Arts Education
- Reimers philosophy of Aesthetic Ed.
- Zoltan Kodály
- Bruner's spiral ciriculum theory to music instruction
- Suzuki methods
- Transfer of learning approach – Prior Knowledge
- Vocal Ranges

- Dalcrose
- Philosophy of music Ed (↑ comprehensive musicianship)

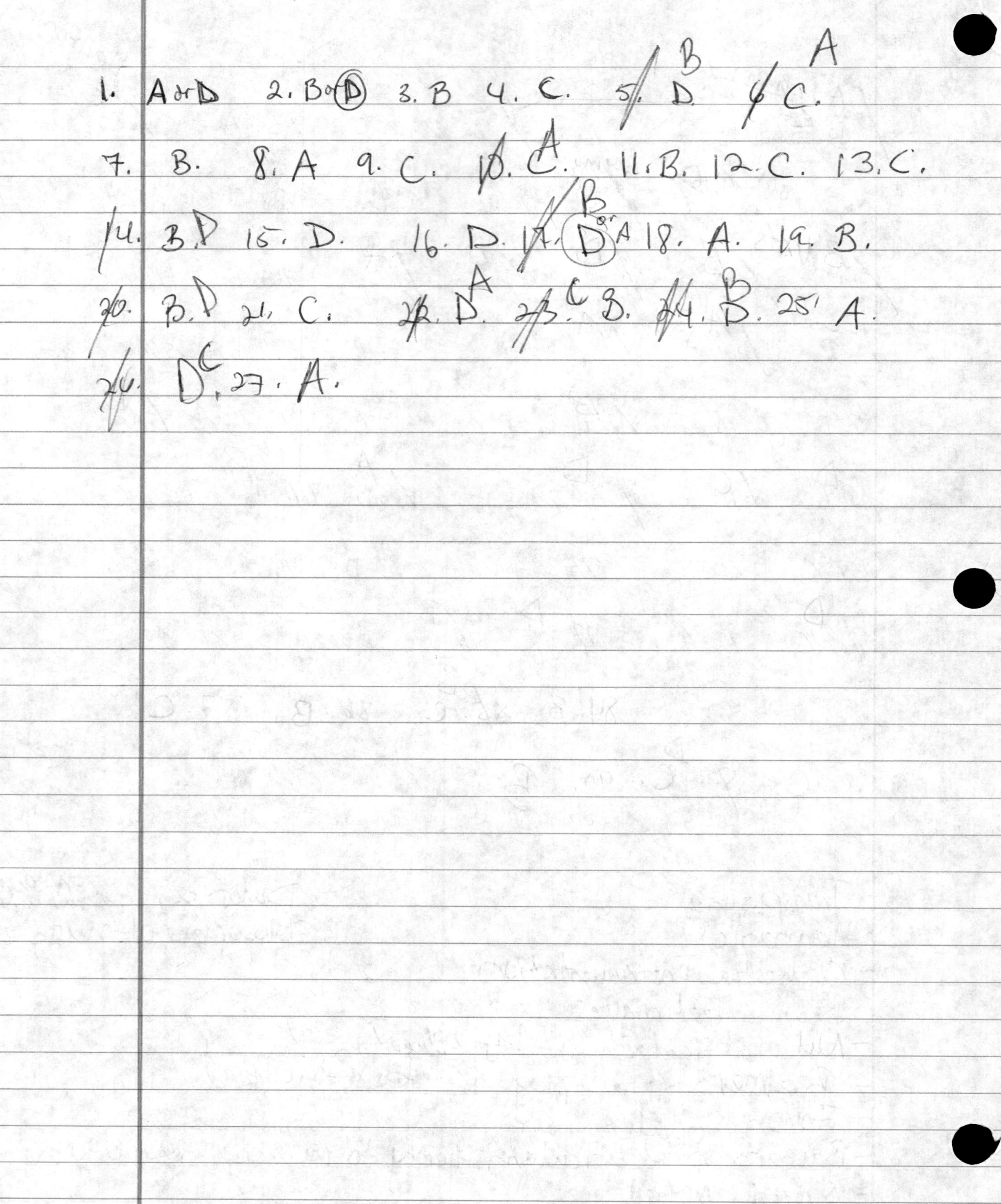

1. A or D 2. B or (D) 3. B 4. C. 5. D. [B above] 6. C. [A above]

7. B. 8. A 9. C. 10. C. [A above] 11. B. 12. C. 13. C.

14. B. D 15. D. 16. D. 17. (D) [B or A] 18. A. 19. B.

20. B. D 21. C. 22. D. [A above] 23. B. [C above] 24. D. [B above] 25. A.

26. D. [C above] 27. A.

48. Which of the following is an application of Bruner's spiral curriculum theory to music instruction?

(A) Fifth-grade students learn a song by rote; then they learn the song with syllables by rote; then they learn to read the song in notation.
(B) Third-grade students sing a song; then they add instrumental accompaniment to the song; then they add movement to the song.
(C) First-grade students learn about up-and-down melodic motion; in third grade they learn about melodic motion by steps and leaps; in fifth grade they learn to distinguish between thirds and fifths in a melodic contour.
(D) First-grade students learn to sing songs less than two minutes long; in fifth grade they learn to sing songs four minutes long; in ninth grade they learn to sing multiple-movement works more than nine minutes long

49. Beginning brass players often play with a closed throat and oral cavity to compensate for

(A) inadequate breath support
(B) a mouthpiece that is too big
(C) a poor embouchure
(D) a tongue that is arched too high

50. The arrangers Hall Johnson, William Dawson, and Jester Hairston are associated with which of the following genres?

(A) Spirituals
(B) Musical comedy
(C) Jazz
(D) Rhythm and blues

51. Which of the following pieces would be most useful for introducing the instruments of the orchestra to elementary general music students?

(A) *Tubby the Tuba*
(B) *Night on Bald Mountain*
(C) *Peter and the Wolf*
(D) *Babar the Elephant*

52. All of the following are benefits of portfolio assessment in music education EXCEPT:

(A) It permits an assessment of student learning over time.
(B) It accommodates student creativity.
(C) It is less time-consuming than other forms of assessment.
(D) It can be used with an integrated arts approach.

53. If a school district subscribes to Gardner's theory of multiple intelligences, which of the following would best describe music's place in the curriculum?

(A) Music is taught as a core subject.
(B) Music is taught to students with high aptitude.
(C) Music is taught only at the secondary level.
(D) Music is an extracurricular course offering.

54. Which of the following is the most appropriate sequence for teaching a music concept in a general music class?

(A) Preparation, extension, practice, presentation
(B) Practice, preparation, presentation, extension
(C) Preparation, presentation, practice, extension
(D) Presentation, extension, preparation, practice

55. Which of the following has the richest instructional potential for an integrated arts unit?

(A) Electronic music
(B) Musical theater
(C) Program music
(D) Oratorio

56. Which of the following is the most appropriate kinesthetic activity for demonstrating an understanding of pitch?

(A) Using hand signs
(B) Identifying the half steps and whole steps in a scale by name
(C) Labeling solfège syllables
(D) Performing a song from memory

57. All of the following are important to the pedagogical approach of Shin'ichi Suzuki EXCEPT

(A) beginning instruction at an early age
(B) reading music at an early age
(C) performing in groups
(D) parental involvement

58. Which of the following statements best describes musical instrument digital interface (MIDI) ?

(A) The computer language that enables computers and electronic musical instruments to "speak" to each other
(B) A hardware device connected to a computer that stores large amounts of audio information
(C) A software program designed to work with synthesizers
(D) A system for recording analog sound

59. High school students are most likely to accept classroom rules when the students

(A) like the teacher
(B) are afraid of the teacher
(C) have a voice in making the rules
(D) like the subject being taught

60. Which of the following is the most appropriate music instructional objective for teaching the music of a non-Western culture in a United States middle school music class?

(A) The students will look up information about the culture's history.
(B) The students will gain a respect for the religious traditions of the culture.
(C) The students will recognize and be able to describe the characteristic sounds of the music.
(D) The students will transcribe pieces using Western notation.

61. Which of the following represents an application of the transfer of learning approach in a high school choral class?

(A) The students listen to a recording of a new piece before attempting to sing it.
(B) The students clap the rhythm of a new piece before attempting to sing it.
(C) The students sing the melody of a new piece on a neutral syllable before singing the text.
(D) The students recall musical features of familiar music that are present in a new piece before attempting to sing it.

62. Of the following, which musical task requires students to use the highest level of cognitive processing?

(A) Labeling given notation as "quarter note," "eighth note," "triplet," etc.
(B) Placing the bar lines correctly in a series of rhythmically notated pitches, given a particular meter signature
(C) Labeling the beats with numbers in a measured rhythmic example for which meter and bar lines are given
(D) Using several rhythmic note values to write a four-measure rhythmic pattern in a given meter

63. Which of the following ranges is NOT typical of the voices of high school students?

64. All of the following are considered basic to Dalcroze instruction EXCEPT

(A) solfège
(B) improvisation
(C) eurhythmics
(D) harmonization

The following question is based on the score printed below.

65. The methodology in which such score usage occurs is

(A) Orff-Schulwerk
(B) Dalcroze eurhythmics
(C) Manhattanville Music Curriculum Project
(D) Music in Education

66. Which of the following techniques would be most appropriate for achieving the proper vocal tone from an elementary school chorus?

    (A) Vocal modeling
    (B) Study sheets
    (C) Diagrams illustrating vocal production
    (D) Playing the vocal lines on the piano

67. Which of the following gives the most essential minimum requirements of an elementary school music program?

    (A) Vocal classes for all students
    (B) General music classes for all students and elective programs and performance groups for interested students
    (C) Keyboard classes for all students and string and instrumental groups for interested students
    (D) Music appreciation and instrumental classes for all students

68. A high school choir may have difficulty sight-singing the melody above because

    (A) there is no text
    (B) the rhythms are complex
    (C) the tonic is not clearly established
    (D) the range is too wide

69. By the completion of grade 4, most students in the general music program should be able to

(A) sing a two-octave scale with complete accuracy
(B) sing or play melodies in treble or bass clef at sight
(C) sing a repertoire of folk and composed songs from memory
(D) improvise harmonic accompaniments for recorded music

70. Which of the following is the LEAST appropriate activity for inclusion in an integrated arts unit?

(A) Learning how music, poetry, and dance are combined in Mozart's *Magic Flute*
(B) Showing how repetition, contrast, and balance are common to music and the visual arts
(C) Comparing and contrasting 12-bar blues form with Classical sonata form
(D) Analyzing different representations of nature in a specific piece of music, a painting, and a poem

71. Experience in learning songs by rote contributes most to which of the following?

(A) Extending vocal range
(B) Developing aural skills
(C) Developing musical independence
(D) Increasing ensemble performance skills

72. Once a student understands intervals, the most logical next step in a learning sequence in music theory is

(A) harmonic rhythm
(B) voice-leading
(C) triads
(D) nonchord tones

73. In selecting repertoire for listening lessons, the teacher should primarily choose music that

(A) has immediate appeal for the students
(B) is composed by living composers
(C) spans the widest possible range of musical periods
(D) provides examples of concepts being studied in class

74. The study of music elements provides a framework for music learning. These elements are

(A) melody, harmony, rhythm, timbre, texture, form
(B) melody, rhythm, scales, expression, form, dynamics
(C) form, dynamics, feeling, emotion, rhythm, tempo
(D) notation, symbols, performance, emotion, interpretation, context

75. What should be the first step in the process of curriculum development in music?

(A) Sequencing music-learning tasks
(B) Identifying goals and objectives
(C) Purchasing music and equipment
(D) Selecting appropriate music literature

76. Grades in a general music class are most appropriately based on the students'

(A) improvement in attitude toward music
(B) development of aesthetic preferences
(C) increased musical aptitude
(D) mastery of instructional objectives

77. A student is asked to identify the features of a piece of music that indicate its style period. In which of the following domains would this task best be categorized?

(A) Cognitive
(B) Affective
(C) Attitude
(D) Psychomotor

78. The musical arrangement for SATB chorus that is easiest to sing is one in which

(A) the melodic motives are imitated in each part
(B) the rhythmic organization is varied and features syncopation
(C) slow-moving block chords are performed *divisi* in eight parts
(D) each part moves diatonically within a limited range and dynamic level

79. Which of the following arrangers has written most extensively for high school strings?

(A) Joyce Eilers
(B) Sandra Dackow
(C) Sammy Nestico
(D) Jay Bocook

80. In what method or approach to sight singing is the note C always sung "do"?

(A) Fixed do
(B) Moveable do
(C) Tonic sol-fa
(D) Solfeggio

81. Which of the following is an appropriate instrument-care objective for beginning string orchestra students to master?

(A) Students should loosen the hair on the bow before returning it to the case.
(B) Students should loosen the tuning pegs on the instrument before returning it to the case.
(C) Students should wipe the rosin from the bow hair before returning it to the case.
(D) Students should put rosin on the bow before returning it to the case.

82. Which of the following objectives is most appropriate for the first lessons in an introductory, hands-on music technology unit in the elementary classroom?

(A) Students will explain differences between Moog synthesizers and MIDI technology.
(B) Students will select a timbre on a synthesizer and use it to create simple musical patterns.
(C) Students will make live microphone recordings of their own performances.
(D) Students will compose and orchestrate a 3-minute work using at least four different timbres.

83. Which of the following statements is LEAST consistent with a contemporary approach to teaching harmony?

(A) Aural recognition of harmonic techniques should begin with conceptualization of chordal spellings and progressions.
(B) Rock and ethnic folk music offer students an opportunity to analyze and perceive basic harmonic progressions.
(C) Perception of chord changes and progressions can be developed as early as the primary grades.
(D) Aural recognition of modulation can be developed in early middle school students.

PROFESSIONAL PRACTICES

84. Which of the following questions would be most appropriate as the basis for conceptualizing a philosophy of music education?

(A) When will selected literature be taught?
(B) Why should students master musical skills and knowledge?
(C) How will certain musical topics be taught?
(D) What musical selections and other materials should be presented to students?

85. The philosophy of comprehensive musicianship emphasizes the encouragement of

(A) the study of music from around the world
(B) students to function in the various roles of performer, listener, and composer-improviser
(C) a sequential curriculum that focuses on well-defined skill and concept hierarchies for every element of music
(D) the integration of music skills with movement and language development

86. All of the following actions violate the "fair use" guidelines under current United States copyright law EXCEPT:

(A) Copying individual pieces of music from a variety of sources to compile an anthology for instrumental students
(B) Making an emergency copy of a purchased part that one of the band members lost and ordering a replacement copy from the publisher
(C) Copying individual published works for compilation into a workbook to be distributed to the students in a general music class when the textbook budget has been exhausted for the year
(D) Purchasing one score and one set of choral parts of the school musical, then copying 20 extra choral parts so that everyone in the chorus will have his or her own copy

87. All of the following statements concerning the *National Standards for Arts Education* are true EXCEPT:

(A) Standards for dance, music, theatre, and visual arts are included.
(B) The standards were developed with input from many arts educators and several arts education associations.
(C) The standards include detailed lesson plans for teaching basic concepts and skills in the arts.
(D) The standards promote the idea that education in the arts should be available for all students, not just those with special gifts or talents.

88. Which of the following organizations was responsible for promoting arts standards as a part of the national Goals 2000 efforts and finally publishing the *National Standards For Arts Education: What Every Young American Should Know and Be Able to Do in the Arts* (1994) ?

(A) United States Department of Education
(B) The College Music Society
(C) Music Educators National Conference
(D) National Association of Schools of Music

89. In its historical context, the pedagogical debate over teaching music reading by rote versus by a pure reading approach led most directly to which of the following developments in music education?

(A) A child-centered curriculum
(B) A national philosophy of music education
(C) The Suzuki approach to instrumental performance
(D) A questioning of accepted notions concerning the how and why of teaching music

90. According to the *National Standards for Arts Education*, which of the following achievement levels is expected for all students in grades 9–12?

(A) Proficient in all four art forms
(B) Proficient in at least one art form
(C) Advanced in two art forms
(D) Advanced in at least one art form

Chapter 6
Right Answers and Explanations for the *Music: Content Knowledge* Practice Test

► ► ► ► ► ► ► ► ► ► ► ►

Right Answers and Content Categories

Now that you have answered all of the practice questions, you can check your work. Compare your answers with the correct answers in the table below.

Question Number	Correct Answer	Content Category	Question Number	Correct Answer	Content Category
1	D	Music Theory	46	B	Music Learning, K-12
2	D	Music History and Literature	47	A	Music Learning, K-12
3	B	Music History and Literature	48	C	Professional Practices
4	C	Music History and Literature	49	A	Music Learning, K-12
5	B	Music Theory	50	A	Music Learning, K-12
6	A	Music History and Literature	51	C	Music Learning, K-12
7	B	Music Theory	52	C	Music Learning, K-12
8	A	Music History and Literature	53	A	Music Learning, K-12
9	C	Performance	54	C	Music Learning, K-12
10	A	Music History and Literature	55	B	Music Learning, K-12
11	B	Music History and Literature	56	A	Music Learning, K-12
12	C	Music Theory	57	B	Music Learning, K-12
13	C	Music Theory	58	A	Music Learning, K-1
14	D	Music Theory	59	C	Music Learning, K-12
15	D	Music Theory	60	C	Music Learning, K-12
16	D	Performance	61	D	Music Learning, K-12
17	B	Music History and Literature	62	D	Music Learning, K-12
18	A	Music History and Literature	63	C	Music Learning, K-12
19	B	Music Theory	64	D	Music Learning, K-12
20	D	Music Theory	65	A	Music Learning, K-12
21	C	Music History and Literature	66	A	Music Learning, K-12
22	A	Music Theory	67	B	Music Learning, K-12
23	C	Music History and Literature	68	C	Music Learning, K-12
24	B	Music Theory	69	C	Music Learning, K-12
25	A	Performance	70	C	Music Learning, K-12
26	C	Performance	71	B	Music Learning, K-12
27	A	Performance	72	C	Music Learning, K-12
28	A	Performance	73	D	Music Learning, K-12
29	C	Performance	74	A	Music Learning, K-12
30	A	Performance	75	B	Music Learning, K-12
31	C	Performance	76	D	Music Learning, K-12
32	C	Performance	77	A	Music Learning, K-12
33	A	Performance	78	D	Music Learning, K-12
34	C	Performance	79	B	Music Learning, K-12
35	C	Music History and Literature	80	A	Music Learning, K-12
36	D	Performance	81	A	Music Learning, K-12
37	A	Performance	82	B	Music Learning, K-12
38	B	Performance	83	A	Music Learning, K-12
39	B	Performance	84	B	Professional Practices
40	C	Performance	85	B	Professional Practices
41	B	Music Learning, K-12	86	B	Professional Practices
42	B	Professional Practices	87	C	Professional Practices
43	D	Music Learning, K-12	88	C	Professional Practices
44	D	Music Learning, K-12	89	D	Professional Practices
45	A	Music Learning, K-12	90	B	Professional Practices

Explanations of Right Answers

Section I (questions on excerpts from the CD)

Most of the following explanations contain one or more italicized terms or names. As a study technique, look up the terms or names and study the concepts, history, and repertoire associated with them.

1. This question tests your ability to identify the *texture* of this musical excerpt and your understanding of texture terms. The texture of this excerpt consists of chords played in a chorale style, so the correct answer is *homophony*. The correct answer is, therefore, (D).

2. This question asks you to analyze the stylistic elements in the recorded excerpt to select the period that the excerpt best represents. The style of the phrasing, texture, harmony, and *orchestration* are indicative of *Impressionism*. The correct answer is, therefore, (D).

3. This question tests your knowledge of world music. The instrumentation, the subtle *rhythm*, phrase length, and melodic embellishments are indicative of the *music of India*. The correct answer is, therefore, (B).

4. This question tests your knowledge of the specific genre. This passage from *Bach's* "Liebster Jesu" is a typical example of a *chorale prelude*. The correct answer is, therefore, (C).

5. This question asks you to analyze the excerpt harmonically. The excerpt, an *exposition* from the first movement of a Classical sonata, begins in the *tonic* and ends in the *dominant*. The correct answer, therefore, is (B).

6. This question tests your ability to match the composer with an excerpt of his work. If you were not familiar with the composer or the work, then an analysis of the *style characteristics* of the piece would allow you conclude that the piece was representative of the *Classical Period*. The only Classical composer is *Mozart*. The correct answer is, therefore, (A).

7. This question tests your knowledge of musical and expressive devices and your ability to recognize them in performance. The beginning of this excerpt is characterized by a gradual increase in tempo. This tempo increase could be appropriately marked *accelerando*. The correct answer is, therefore, (B).

8. This question tests your ability to match the composer with an excerpt of his work. The harmony, rhythm, and orchestration are typical of *Aaron Copland's* works. The correct answer is, therefore, (A).

9. This question tests your ability to recognize both vocal and instrumental textures. The vocal texture alternates between a *soprano* solo and a chorus. The instrumental accompaniment is a drone. The correct answer, therefore, is (C).

10. This question tests your knowledge of musical chronology. This is an excerpt from "O Jerusalem," by Hildegard of Bingen. Characteristics such as the *modal* melodic lines, lack of a definite meter, and the *drone* are typical of music from around the year *1150*. The correct answer is, therefore, (A).

11. This question tests your familiarity with jazz artists and your ability to recognize their style. This excerpt features the unique sound of *Wynton Marsalis*. The correct answer is, therefore, (B).

12. This question tests your understanding of music theory and your ability to analyze aurally. The interval is a *perfect fourth*. The correct answer is, therefore, (C).

13. This question tests your ability to identify notation aurally. The second phrase begins a fifth higher than the first. The second phrase also uses an *altered* first *scale degree*. The correct answer is therefore, (C).

14. This question tests your knowledge of phrase forms and your ability to recognize them. The form of the phrase is a *parallel double period* with no *extension*. The correct answer is, therefore, (D).

15. This question also tests your knowledge of *phrase structure* and how analyses of such structures may be symbolized using letters. The part (a) is repeated with a slight rhythmic change (a'). These are followed by a contrasting phrase (b) that is repeated at a higher pitch level (b'). Therefore, (D) is the correct answer.

16. This question tests your ability to analyze the rhythmic structure of the excerpt to determine the most appropriate *beat pattern*. The most appropriate pattern is an *asymmetrical* three beat pattern with a long first beat (*subdivided* by 3), followed by two shorter beats (each subdivided by 2). The correct answer, therefore, is (D).

17. This question tests your knowledge of world music. The rhythms and unique vocal style indicate music of an *American Woodland Indian culture* of North America. The correct answer is, therefore, (B).

18. This question asks you to analyze the musical characteristics of this style and select the appropriate country of origin. The rhythm, instrumentation, vocal parts, and unique fusion of *big band, Latino,* and *African* elements are characteristic of the *mambo*, a popular dance music that originated in Cuba. The correct answer is, therefore, (A).

19. This question tests your knowledge of music theory and your ability to analyze the quality of chords. The *triad* played is minor. The correct answer is, therefore, (B).

20. This question tests your ability to analyze phrase structure. The excerpt presents a second phrase that contrasts in harmonic and *melodic material* with the first phrase. Therefore, the correct answer is (D).

21. This question requires you to analyze the characteristics of the excerpt and select the period it represents. The instrument—the piano—the rubato tempo, thick and lush harmony, and the strong emotional content suggest the *Romantic Period*. The correct answer is, therefore, (C).

22. This question tests your knowledge of *rhythmic devices*. Because the rhythm of the flute part emphasizes off beats, syncopation (A) is the correct answer. Although hemiola (changing from a meter of 2 groups of 3 to one of 3 groups of 2 or vice versa) can be a considered a kind of syncopation, no hemiola is present in the example.

23. This question tests your familiarity with the history and characteristics of popular music. The vocal techniques and accompaniment style are typical characteristics of early rock 'n' roll. The correct answer is, therefore, (C).

24. This question tests your knowledge of music theory and your ability to analyze the quality of chords. The *arpeggio* played is a descending minor seventh. The correct answer is, therefore, (B).

25. This question tests your ability to identify specific instrumental techniques in performance. The unique sound heard in the snare drum part is produced by the *rim shot*. The correct answer is, therefore, (A).

26. This question tests your ability to identify performance errors. An examination of the score shows that the eighth notes are to remain equal through the meter changes (see the marking above measure 3). The eighth notes in measure 3, however, are played too fast (as if they were triplets in the original tempo) at the meter change. The correct answer is, therefore, (C).

27. This question tests your ability to identify performance errors and to interpret a score correctly. The chorus does not observe the dynamic indicating a decrescendo. Therefore, the correct answer is (A).

Section II (non-CD section)

28. Alto saxophones are pitched in E-flat—one whole step lower than horns in F. To accommodate the difference, the horn part would need to be transposed down one whole step and the key signature would have to be adjusted by taking away two sharps. The correct answer is, therefore, (A).

29. Typically, the harmonic progression ("changes") is more likely to remain constant as various performers improvise. The number of performers playing at any given time would likely vary due to entrances, exits, and combinations of instruments. The ornamentation of the melody inevitably varies with the improvisation of each soloist; and the tessitura of the various solo instruments or voices also is likely to differ. The correct answer is, therefore, (C).

30. The tenor part is indicated by the T in the score to the left of the second staff from the bottom. The text below the line gives this away as a vocal line. The tenor clef identifies the fourth line as middle C. The lowest pitch is in the third bar and is an F#. The correct answer is, therefore, (A).

31. The English horn is a transposing instrument in F, written a fifth above the concert pitch. The correct answer is, therefore, (C).

32. The most appropriate sequence of conducting patterns is determined by the number of beats in each bar, the tempo, and the pattern of accents. The example should first be conducted in three because of the tempo marking (quarter note = 60). The second measure should be conducted in a three-plus-two pattern of five beats because of the accents. The third measure should be conducted in three and the last measure in four. The correct answer is, therefore, (C).

33. The dynamics, date of composition, or the form of the music is unlikely to have any bearing on the appropriate conducting pattern of measures written in five-eight meter. The appropriate conducting pattern depends mostly on the tempo of the piece. The correct answer is, therefore, (A).

34. The harmonic (or overtone) series begins with a fundamental, a B-flat in this case. The first partial (overtone) is an octave higher and the next is a fifth above in this case F. The correct answer is, therefore, (C).

35. Although it is common today for performers to use composed cadenzas, performers were expected to improvise their own cadenzas during the eighteenth and nineteenth centuries. The authentic performance practice movement has led to some revival of improvised cadenzas. The correct answer is, therefore, (C).

36. The presence of the clarinet, the repeated figure in the low strings, and the style of short, regular phrases suggest the Classical style. The four-part chorus (coro in Italian) is written on three staves: the soprano and alto are combined on the first, the tenor on the second, and the bass on the third. The correct answer is, therefore, (D).

37. The arrowheads above the notes indicate the martelé bowing technique. The correct answer is, therefore, (A).

38. Performing the dotted half note (a larger value) as fast as the half note (a lesser value) speeds up the tempo and shortens the value of the half note. The correct answer is, therefore, (B).

39. Clues such as the alto clef in the third staff and the double notes not marked divisi suggest a four-part string ensemble with one instrument playing each part. The score format is typical of a string quartet. The correct answer is, therefore, (B).

40. The *preparatory beat* in conducting must establish the tempo and dynamic of the attack. The correct answer is, therefore, (C).

41. The *National Standards for Arts Education* are a consensus-based outline of outcomes for music students in grades 4, 8, and 12. The correct answer is, therefore, (B).

42. *Reimer's* philosophy advocates that all students be actively involved in the music activities of listening, composing, and performing. The correct answer is, therefore, (B).

43. The *Kodály method* focuses on singing and the development of the voice. The correct answer is, therefore, (D).

44. Asking to hear the piece again is the only *affective* student response given. The correct answer is, therefore, (D).

45. Morley is known for the quality and quantity of *madrigals* that are *appropriate for high school* students. The correct answer is, therefore, (A).

46. CD-ROM multimedia software is an effective tool in developing music skills through *interactive learning*. The correct answer is, therefore, (B).

47. The *sequence* in which children develop a sense of pitch begins with the ability to distinguish between high and low sounds. This is followed by the ability to distinguish basic melodic contours—up and down. The ability to specifically identify step or skip movement follows. The correct answer is, therefore, (A).

48. *Bruner's spiral curriculum theory* can be demonstrated using development of melodic contour as an example. The correct answer is, therefore, (C).

49. Beginning students on woodwind and brass instruments commonly restrict the throat and oral cavity, to compensate for poor breath support, thus producing a weak, thin sound. Similarly, *poor breath support* can cause young singers to sing too much in the throat and head, causing a weak sound. The correct answer is, therefore, (A).

50. Hall Johnson, William Dawson, and Jester Hairston are arrangers of spirituals *appropriate for middle and senior high school-aged vocal ensembles*. The correct answer is, therefore, (A).

51. *Peter and the Wolf*, the symphonic fairy tale by Prokofiev, depicts characters through various instruments. Familiarity with the sounds of the instruments in the story would provide the foundation for *introducing orchestral instruments* to elementary grade students. The correct answer is, therefore, (C).

52. This question asks you discern which option is NOT a benefit of portfolio assessment. Portfolio *assessment* is usually more time-consuming to construct and evaluate than other forms of assessment, in part because a wide variety of skills and accomplishments are combined in a personalized presentation. The correct answer is, therefore, (C).

53. Gardner's theory includes music as one of the *multiple intelligences* that should be addressed as a *core subject*. The correct answer is, therefore, (A).

54. Music concepts should be prepared through various musical experiences prior to the formal presentation of the concept. Then the students should be given opportunities to use and practice this new knowledge. As students gain confidence and competence, opportunities to *extend learning* should be provided. The correct answer is, therefore, (C).

55. Musical theater provides *integrated arts* learning opportunities for students to study drama, dance, costume, set design, as well as music. The correct answer is, therefore, (B).

56. The only *kinesthetic* activity provided as an option is using hand signs. The other choices are aural or visual activities. The correct answer is, therefore, (A).

57. The *Suzuki* pedagogical approach does not promote music reading at an early age. Instead, the approach develops musical ability through aural and rote learning in a manner similar to language acquisition. The correct answer is, therefore, (B).

58. Choice (A) gives the correct definition of *MIDI*.

59. When high school students are involved in the establishment of the *classroom rules*, they are more accepting of the rules regardless of their opinion of the teacher or the subject being taught. The correct answer is, therefore, (C).

60. An appropriate music *instructional objective* would be for students to focus on the representative characteristics of the music. The correct answer is, therefore, (C).

61. To transfer learning, students must apply what they have already learned to a new situation. Recalling musical features of familiar music in a new piece demonstrates transfer of learning from the familiar to the new. The correct answer is, therefore, (D).

62. Writing a four-measure rhythmic pattern demonstrates synthesis that is a *high-order cognitive ability*. The other answer choices involve identification and comprehension, which are lower-level cognitive processing skills. The correct answer is, therefore, (D).

63. The range expressed in answer choice (C) is too high for the high school tenor voice.

64. *Dalcroze* involves the student and teacher in solfège, improvisation, and eurhythmics. Harmonization is generally not considered basic to Dalcroze instruction. The correct answer is, therefore, (D).

65. The score is typical of *Orff-Schulwerk* in which various instruments are layered to create an ensemble experience for the students. The correct answer is, therefore, (A).

66. The correct answer is (A). For elementary students to achieve proper tone quality, they need to have direct experience with appropriate vocal timbres in comparison to their own, such as by modeling their tone after that produced by a vocalist-teacher. Worksheets and diagrams do not provide a suitable aural comparison of a desirable tone quality versus an undesirable tone quality. Playing vocal lines on the piano can provide students with a musical model of, for example, a melodic shape, but not of vocal tone.

67. The correct answer is (B). General music classes for elementary students, especially for grades K-4, establish an important foundation for further specialized studies at later grade levels. Vocal classes, keyboard classes, and instrumental groups are valuable experiences that are best started after students have been introduced to music through a quality general music curriculum.

68. Because of the large number of accidentals, the melody does not have a clear tonal center, which makes it difficult for high school students to sight-sing. Melodies without text are not more difficult for students to sight-read. The range of the melody is appropriate for high school singers and, with the slight exception of the tie in measure 3, the rhythms in the melody are simple. The correct answer, therefore, is (C).

69. According to the *National Standards for Arts Education,* students at grade 4 should be able to sing a varied repertoire of songs, including some by memory, with expression and appropriate dynamics, phrasing, and interpretation. The other skills listed (singing a two-octave scale, performing melodies by sight in bass or treble clef, and improvising harmonic accompaniments) are above the expectations for fourth grade students. The correct answer, therefore, is (C).

70. The correct answer is (C). Integrated arts units seek to incorporate the study of more than one art form (e.g., music, theatre, visual arts, dance). Comparing two musical forms (e.g., 12-bar blues and Classical sonata form) does not allow for the inclusion of another art form. However, studying the *Magic Flute*, studying various types of art that use the theme of "repetition," and analyzing different depictions of nature each allow the study of at least one other art form in addition to music.

71. Learning songs by rote allows students to develop their "musical memory," which helps them to perceive musical patterns aurally. The goals of extending vocal ranges, developing musical independence, and increasing ensemble performance skills are best developed with targeted exercises that are relatively unrelated to learning songs by rote. The correct answer, therefore, is (B).

72. After students learn intervals, the next most logical step would be for them to study triads by building on the knowledge of the intervals of thirds and fifths. Nonchord tones, voice-leading, and harmonic rhythms are best taught after students have mastered triads and other chords, such as seventh chords. The correct answer, therefore, is (C).

73. There is real value in using music that has immediate appeal, including music of living composers. Use of music from a wide span of periods can also be helpful. But they are not the most important factors to consider when implementing a curriculum. Teachers who seek to implement a sequential music curriculum first consider the concepts that should be taught, and then locate repertoire from which to teach those concepts. The correct answer, therefore, is (D).

74. The correct answer is (A), which provides a list of musical elements. Concepts such as "expression," "tempo," "scales," and "notation" are not elements of music by themselves, but are studied as a natural outgrowth of one or more musical elements.

75. The most logical first step in curriculum development is first to determine the key learning goals and objectives for a given classroom. After developing learning goals and objectives, the teacher may select repertoire, develop sequenced lesson plans, and determine music and equipment needs. The correct answer, therefore, is (B).

76. The correct answer is (D). The primary goal of musical instruction in a general music class is to present a sequential music curriculum for which students should demonstrate mastery. The development of improved attitudes toward music and the development of musical preferences are laudable outcomes as a result of classroom instruction. But they do not constitute the core skills and knowledge upon which students should be graded. Musical aptitude is, by definition, the measured potential for students to learn in music and is not part of music curriculum.

77. The options given relate to Bloom's taxonomy, originally outlined in the 1950s to describe three domains, or categories, of educational behavior: cognitive (knowledge- or mind-based); affective (relating to attitudes, appreciations, or values); and psychomotor (based on manual or physical skills). The correct answer is (A), because the task mainly requires applying knowledge to solve a problem. For an application of the taxonomy to music education, see Harold F. Abeles, Charles R. Hoffer, and Robert H. Klotman, *Foundations of Music Education*, 2nd ed. (New York: Schirmer Books/Wadsworth Publishing Company, 1995), pp. 233-41.

78. The best answer is (D), because it does not present any particular challenges for the singers. The other choices all imply some degree of challenge that makes the works more difficult than (D). Specifically, (A) employs polyphony, (B) has rhythmic challenges, and (C) requires singing in more than four parts.

79. Eilers is a choral arranger, Nestico is a band arranger, and Bocook composes and arranges for band. Dackow, on the other hand, arranges primarily for string and full orchestra. The correct answer, therefore, is (B).

80. C is always sung "do" in fixed do, regardless of the music's tonal center. In movable do, tonic sol-fa, and solfeggio, the first scale degree is always "do." The correct answer, therefore, is (A).

81. The only choice that is appropriate is (A). This is necessary to prevent the bow stick from being damaged by undue tension. Loosening the tuning pegs to release the string tension, on the other hand, is inadvisable because it may cause additional wear on the strings and the instrument. Rosin is applied *before* playing to help produce a good tone. After every use, loose rosin dust should be wiped from the bow stick, instrument, and strings—but definitely not the bow hairs.

82. At the elementary level, students are introduced to timbre and other elements of music. They begin to create short songs and instrumental pieces, using synthesizers if they are available. The correct answer, therefore, is (B). For an introductory, hands-on unit at this level, students should not be expected to be able to explain either MIDI technology or the Moog synthesizer. Making live microphone recordings might be desirable in some situations (for example, if students were recording their own short compositions), but it would not be applicable for a hands-on music technology unit. (D) would not necessarily involve music technology, and the task would not be appropriate for the stated purpose.

83. Of the choices, (A) is the least in keeping with a contemporary approach to teaching harmony. Edwin Gordon, for example, contends that introducing students to theoretical understanding before they can discriminate music aurally can hinder development of abilities such as improvising and performing with proper intonation and rhythm. [See Edwin Gordon, *Learning Sequences in Music: Skill, Content, and Patterns*, 7th ed. (Chicago, IL: GIA Publications, 1997), pp. 133–34.] (B) would be dependent upon the particular rock or ethnic folk music that was being used. (C) and (D) relate to the issue of readiness, rather than to the approach or sequence to be used. The correct answer, therefore, is (A).

84. The answer to the question of *why musical skills and knowledge are mastered* provides the basis for answering the other questions of when, how, and what literature, topics, selections, and materials should be presented. The correct answer is, therefore, (B).

85. *Comprehensive musicianship* seeks to develop musical understanding and skills directly through student participation in all the roles of a musician: performer, listener, and composer. The correct answer is, therefore, (B).

86. Copying for emergency replacement of music, provided that another copy is ordered from the publisher, meets the criteria for *fair use* regarding *copyright law*. The other examples are in violation. The correct answer is, therefore, (B).

87. The *Standards* serve as a guideline for what students should be able to do at different grade levels but do not provide detailed *lesson plans* for accomplishing this. The correct answer is, therefore, (C).

88. The Music Educators National Conference (MENC) was directly responsible for the inclusion of the arts standards in the national *Goals 2000*. MENC also established nine national standards for music education and developed guidelines based on these nine standards for grades 4, 8, and 12, and published these with the other Arts Education programs in *National Standards For Arts Education: What Every Young American Should Know and Be Able to Do in the Arts* (1994). The correct answer is, therefore, (C).

89. By the 1880s, schools were beginning to address the issue of music as entertainment versus music as an educational experience. [See Michael L. Mark and Charles E. Gary, *A History of American Music Education*, 2nd ed. (Reston, VA: MENC, 1999), p. 180.] In the decades that followed, this led to debate about the need for music specialists, appropriate pedagogical methods for sight-reading, and the rationale for music education. The correct answer, therefore, is (D). The other choices are incorrect because the nation does not adhere to a specific philosophy of music education; the idea of a child-centered curriculum does not relate to the debate specified in the question; and the Suzuki approach was developed in Japan, separate from this debate. With Suzuki in America, (C) could be considered to be subsumed by (D); but the method did not grow out of the stated pedagogical debate.

90. The correct answer is (B). The advanced level may be reached by students who complete courses involving relevant skills and knowledge for three to four years beyond grade 8. But the Standards do not specify that all students must achieve that level in at least one of the arts. See Music Educators National Conference, *The School Music Program—A New Vision: The K-12 National Standards, PreK Standards, and What They Mean to Music Educators* (Reston, VA: MENC, 1994), p. 21.

Chapter 7
Constructed-Response Tests and How Your Responses Will Be Scored

► ► ► ► ► ► ► ► ► ► ► ►

Advice from the Experts

Scorers who have scored hundreds of real tests were asked to give advice to students taking the *Music* constructed response tests. The scorers' advice boils down to the practical pieces of advice given below.

1. **Read through the question carefully before you answer it, and try to answer all parts of the question.**

   This seems simple, but many test takers fail to understand the question and provide a complete response. If the question asks for three activities, don't forget to discuss three. If the question asks for problems and solutions, don't describe just problems. No matter how well you write about *one* part of the question, the scorers cannot award you full credit unless you answer the question completely and correctly.

2. **Show that you understand both the subject-matter concepts related to the question and how to teach them.**

   The scorers are looking to see not only that you understand the musical concepts related to the questions but also that you can apply this knowledge through appropriate strategies to music education situations. You can show you understand these concepts not by merely mentioning that the concepts exist, but by explaining them as you would to students and relating them to the specifics of your response.

   For example, in answering a question about melodic contour, you should not merely restate that every melody has a specific contour; this only repeats the question's text and would not illuminate the concept for your students. You should explain that an understanding of melodic contour is dependent upon the ability to identify the direction of pitches as getting higher, lower, or remaining static. You could also improve on this answer by providing specific examples of melodies appropriate for the age level you are addressing and by demonstrating melodic contours with examples, if the question asks for them, from at least two different musical traditions.

3. **Show that you have a thorough understanding of the specific terms and musical material in the question.**

   Some answers receive partial credit because they are vague—they address the topic at too general a level rather than at a level that takes into consideration the particulars implied by the musical terms or examples.

   Example #1: *The question asks you to demonstrate your knowledge about texture.* Do not make vague references about texture in general, such as the fact that all music has texture, but instead focus on the basic principles of texture—for example, by discussing the different types of texture, by describing different aspects of texture, and by using and explaining appropriate terms such as monophonic, homophonic, and polyphonic.

   Example #2: *The question asks you about teaching the concept of texture in a general music class.* Don't answer the question in terms of texture in *general*, such as stating that a teacher should mention that all music has texture. Instead, focus on a specific definition of texture and communicate an understanding of this definition through strategies and techniques used in a general music class that would contribute to student learning. Discuss a few of the basic types of texture, using appropriate terms such as monophonic, homophonic, and polyphonic, and provide appropriate musical material demonstrating each, such as the melody line from a familiar folksong, a four-part hymn, and a Bach fugue.

A thorough answer also provides the scorer with evidence that you know the specific terms and musical materials related to the questions. Do not simply use the musical terms in a generic sentence that could work for any number of terms. Convince the scorers that you understand the terms and can apply them in appropriate instructional situations.

4. **Support your answers with appropriate details.**

The scorers are looking for justification of your answers. Support your answer with details that demonstrate your level of understanding, and with materials asked for in the question (e.g., musical examples or solutions to common performance problems) that are appropriate for the age level.

By providing appropriate details, examples, and additional information, you help to clarify answers that may be unusual or may be interpreted in other ways.

A word of caution: Superfluous writing will obscure your points and will make it difficult for the scorers to be confident of your full understanding of the material. Be straightforward in your response. Do not try to impress the scorers. If you do not know the answer, you cannot receive full credit, but if you do know the answer, provide enough information to convince the scorers that you have a full understanding of the topic.

5. **Do not change the question or challenge the basis of the question.**

Stay focused on the question that is asked, and do your best to answer it. You will receive no credit or, at best, a low score if you choose to answer another question or if you state, for example, that there is no possible answer.

Answer the question by addressing the fundamental issues. Do not venture off-topic to demonstrate your particular field of expertise if it is not specifically related to the question. This undermines the impression that you understand the concept adequately.

6. **Wherever applicable, demonstrate that you understand, in addition to the basic musical concepts and terms, the concepts related to the instructional needs of the students.**

This may be a description of an appropriate instructional sequence, including the use of appropriate activities and musical materials or examples to teach a basic concept or an aspect of performance technique. In describing an instructional sequence, ensure that all appropriate components have been addressed and arranged in the most logical order. Select music activities, musical materials, and musical examples that will help to clarify the concept for the students, that are appropriate for the age level you are addressing, and that build understanding sequentially.

Test takers sometimes lose points by describing a jumble of activities lacking any sense of direction, although the individual activities might be appropriate. Be sure that you describe a genuine instructional sequence in which each successive activity builds better understanding.

7. Reread your response to check that you have written what you thought you wrote.

Frequently, sentences are left unfinished or clarifying information is omitted. Check for correct use and spelling of all musical terms.

General Scoring Guide for the *Music: Concepts and Processes* (0111) Test

The following guide provides the overarching framework for scoring the questions in the *Music: Concepts and Processes* test.

Music: Concepts and Processes—General Scoring Guide

The scoring of each response will be based on how well it

- demonstrates understanding of the musical concepts and processes presented by the question
- presents musical concepts and strategies for skill development in a pedagogically sound sequence
- answers all parts of the question
- cites or describes grade-level-appropriate musical examples that demonstrate important aspects of the topic posed by the question and that represent a variety of cultural origins and musical traditions; use musical terms accurately; and spell them correctly

Score	Comment
5	▪ demonstrates full understanding of the musical concepts and processes presented by the question ▪ presents musical concepts and strategies for skill development in a sequence that is pedagogically sound ▪ correctly and thoroughly answers all parts of the question ▪ uses a sufficient number of examples, all of which are appropriate for the age or grade level cited and are representative of a variety of cultural origins and musical traditions ▪ uses all musical terms accurately and spells them correctly
4	▪ demonstrates substantial understanding of the musical concepts and processes presented by the question ▪ presents musical concepts and strategies for skill development in a sequence that is pedagogically sound ▪ answers all parts of the question ▪ uses a sufficient number of examples, most of which are appropriate for the age or grade level cited and are representative of a variety of cultural origins and musical traditions ▪ uses all musical terms accurately and spells them correctly, with few exceptions

3
- demonstrates basic understanding of the musical concepts and processes presented by the question
- presents musical concepts and strategies for skill development in a sequence that is in part pedagogically sound
- provides basically correct answers to the major parts of the question
- uses some examples, most of which are appropriate for the age or grade level cited and are representative of a variety of cultural origins and musical traditions
- uses most musical terms accurately and spells most of them correctly

2
- demonstrates limited understanding of the musical concepts and processes presented by the question
- does not present musical concepts and strategies for skill development in a sequence that is pedagogically sound
- answers only part of the question correctly
- uses some examples, few of which are appropriate for the age or grade level cited or are representative of a variety of cultural origins and musical traditions
- uses few musical terms accurately and spells few of them correctly

1
- demonstrates little or no understanding of the musical concepts and processes presented by the question
- does not present musical concepts and strategies for skill development in a sequence that is pedagogically sound
- does not answer any part of the question correctly but provides some ideas that relate to the question
- uses no examples that are appropriate for the age or grade level cited or are representative of a variety of cultural origins and musical traditions
- does not use musical terms accurately or spell them correctly

0
- demonstrates no understanding of the musical concepts and processes presented by the question
- does not present musical concepts and strategies for skill development in a sequence that is pedagogically sound
- does not answer any part of the question correctly
- uses no examples that are appropriate for the age or grade level cited or are representative of a variety of cultural origins and musical traditions
- does not use musical terms accurately or spell them correctly

General Scoring Guides for the *Music: Analysis* (0112) Test

Questions 1 and 2 in the *Music: Analysis* test are error-detection exercises. They are each scored on a scale of 0 to 5. Questions 3A, 3B, and 3C are scored on a scale of 0 to 10.

Music: Analysis—Scoring Guide for Error-Detection Exercises

Each error (including location and description) equals 1 point

- If the description is an adequate explanation of an error that occurs in the measure(s) indicated, 1 point is awarded.
- If the description is not adequate or is a description of an element that is not in error, no point is awarded.

Music: Analysis—Scoring Guide for Score Analysis

Question 3 in the *Music: Analysis* test is a score-analysis question. Responses are scored on a scale of 0 to 10, as explained below.

Topics A and B: Instrumental Music or Choral Music

The score range is 0 to 10. Points are distributed as follows:

For each excerpt:

- 1 point: 1 point for discussing stylistic influences in the piece
- 2 points: 1 point for each correctly identified, accurately described, significant performance challenge. The challenge must be appropriate for the school level circled.
- 2 points: 1 point for each rehearsal technique described to assist students in meeting each challenge. The challenge must be appropriate for the school level circled.

Points for both excerpts will be added together for the total score.

Topic C: General Music

The score range is 0 to 10. Points are distributed as follows:

For each piece:

- 1 point: 1 point for circling a suitable grade level for each piece and defending the selection
- 1 point: 1 point for discussing stylistic influences in the piece
- 3 points: 1 point for identifying each musical concept and explaining how the piece would be used to teach that concept. The concept and demonstration must be appropriate for the school level circled.

Points for both pieces will be added together for the total score.

The Scoring Process

As you build your skills in writing answers to constructed-response questions, it is important to keep in mind the process used to score the tests. If you understand the process by which experts award your scores, you will have a better context in which to think about your strategies for success.

The scoring session

After each test administration, all Praxis test books are returned to ETS. The multiple-choice answer sheets are scored with the use of scanning machines. *Concepts and Processes* booklets are bundled by test title and sent to the location of the scoring session.

The scoring session usually takes place two weeks after the administration and lasts for two, three, or four days, depending on how many tests need to be scored. Each session is led by a "chief scorer," a highly qualified educator who has many years' experience scoring test questions. All of the remaining scorers are also experienced music teachers and teacher-educators. New scorers are thoroughly trained to understand and use all of the scoring materials. Experienced scorers are retrained, with the same approach, at each session and help to train the new scorers. Experienced scorers provide continuity with past sessions, while new scorers provide fresh perspectives. New scorers ensure that the pool of scorers remains large enough to cover the test's needs throughout the year.

At a typical scoring session, eight to twelve scorers are seated at three to four tables, with any new scorers distributed equally across all tables. One of the scoring leaders, a chief scorer or a table leader, sits at each table. The chief scorer is the person who has overall authority over the scoring session and plays a variety of key roles in training and in ensuring consistent and fair scores. Table leaders assist the chief scorer with these responsibilities.

Preparing to train the scorers

Training scorers is a rigorous process, and it is designed to ensure that each response gets a score that is consistent both with the scores given to other papers and with the overall scoring philosophy and criteria established for the test when it was first designed.

The chief scorers first take the scorers through a review of the "General Scoring Guide," which contains the overall criteria, stated in general terms, for awarding a score. The chief scorers also review and discuss—and, when there are new test questions, make additions to—the "Question-Specific Scoring Guides," which apply the rubrics in the general guide to each specific question on the test. The question-specific guides are not intended to cover every possible response the scorers will see. Rather, they are designed to give enough examples to guide the scorers in making accurate judgments about the variety of answers they will encounter.

To begin identifying appropriate training materials for an individual question, the chief scorers first read through many responses from the bundles of responses to get a sense of the range of the responses. They then choose a set of "benchmarks," typically selecting two responses at each score level for each question. These benchmarks serve as representative examples of the kind of response that meets the criteria of each score level and are the foundation for score standards throughout the session.

The chief scorers then choose a set of test taker responses to serve as "sample" papers. These sample papers represent the wide variety of possible responses that the scorers might see. The sample papers will serve as the basis for practice scoring at the scoring session, so that the scorers can "rehearse" how they will apply the scoring criteria before they begin.

The process of choosing a set of benchmark responses and a set of sample responses is followed systematically for each new question to be scored at the session. After the chief scorers are done with their selections and discussions, the sets they have chosen are photocopied and inserted into the scorers' folders for use in future sessions.

Training the scorers

For each question, the training session proceeds in the same way:

1. All scorers review the General Scoring Guide and the Question-Specific Scoring Guides.

2. All scorers carefully read through the question.

3. The leaders guide the scorers through the set of benchmark responses, explaining in detail why each response received the score it did. Scorers are encouraged to ask questions and share their perspectives. All of the scorers are trained together to ensure uniformity in the application of the scoring criteria.

4. Scorers then practice on the set of samples chosen by the leaders. The leaders poll the scorers on what scores they would award and then lead a discussion to ensure that there is consensus about the scoring criteria and how they are to be applied.

5. When the leaders are confident that the scorers will apply the criteria consistently and accurately, the actual scoring begins.

Quality-control processes

There are a number of procedures that are designed to ensure that the accuracy of scoring is maintained during the scoring session and to ensure that each response receives as many points as the scoring criteria allow. The test books, for example, are designed so that any personal or specific information about the examinee, such as name and test center location, is never seen by the scorers. Additionally, each response is scored twice, with the first scorer's decision hidden from the second scorer. If the two scores for a paper are the same or differ by only one point, the scoring for that paper is considered complete, and the test taker will be awarded the sum of the two scores. If the two scores differ by more than one point, the response is scored by one of the chief scorers and the response's score is revised accordingly.

Another way of maintaining scoring accuracy is through "back-reading." Throughout the session, the chief scorers check a random sample of scores awarded by scorers. If the leader finds that a scorer is not applying the scoring criteria appropriately, that scorer is given more training and his/her scores are checked. The chief scorers also back-read all responses that received scores differing by more than one point to ensure that every appropriate point has been awarded.

Finally, the scoring session is designed so that a number of different scorers contribute to any single test taker's score. This minimizes the effects of a scorer who might score slightly more rigorously or generously than other scorers.

The entire scoring process—standardized benchmarks and samples, general and specific scoring guides, adjudication procedures, back-reading, scorer statistics, and rotation of exams to a variety of scorers—is applied consistently and systematically at every scoring session to ensure comparable scores for each administration and across all administrations of the test.

Chapter 8

Preparing for the *Music: Concepts and Processes* Test

► ► ► ► ► ► ► ► ► ► ► ►

The goal of this chapter is to provide you with strategies for how to read, analyze, and understand the questions on the *Music: Concepts and Processes* test and how to outline and write successful responses. After you are taken through these steps, you also will see actual test taker responses to a question from the test and an expert scorer's explanation of why each response received the score it did.

Introduction to the Question Types

The *Music: Concepts and Processes* test consists of two equally weighted 30-minute constructed-response questions.

The first question offers a choice of two topics, one relating to instrumental music and one to choral music. The test taker is asked to demonstrate an understanding of performance techniques either by describing remedial techniques appropriate for specified performance problems in an ensemble rehearsal setting or by describing correct performance techniques related to vocal or instrumental instruction.

The second question asks the test taker to demonstrate an understanding of a musical concept by designing and describing a step-by-step instructional sequence to introduce a music concept in a general music classroom setting. The test taker is asked to include participatory experiences and musical selections of different cultural origins or musical traditions that would be appropriate for the grade level indicated.

What to Study

Success on this test is not simply a matter of learning more about how to respond to constructed-response questions. It also takes real knowledge of the field. As mentioned above, this test is designed to assess your knowledge of musical concepts and skills, musical development, teaching strategies and rehearsal techniques, music literature, and your ability to present appropriate instruction in a pedagogically sound sequence for experiences in the general music classroom, in individual lessons, and in rehearsal settings. Therefore, it would serve you well to consider the following areas for review.

Instrumental concepts, skills, and rehearsal techniques

Be familiar with the developmental sequence of learning to play an instrument and the common topics that should be addressed, such as the following:

- tone quality
- embouchure
- proper breathing
- posture
- playing position
- articulation
- stick grip
- bowing

Be familiar with common problems instrumental students experience, such as the following, and be able to suggest possible solutions and remedial techniques for each:

- poor tone quality
- poor intonation
- lack of balance
- lack of blend

Choral concepts, skills, and rehearsal techniques

Be familiar with the sequence of vocal development and the common topics that should be addressed, such as the following:

- tone quality
- diction
- proper breathing
- posture

Be familiar with common problems choral students experience, such as the following, and be able to suggest possible solutions and remedial techniques for each:

- poor tone quality
- poor intonation
- lack of balance
- lack of blend
- changing voice

General music concepts, skills, and teaching strategies

Be familiar with the elements of music that provide a framework for conceptual learning about music, and review or prepare sample lessons for introducing specific aspects of each: melody, harmony, rhythm, timbre, texture, and form.

Know specific titles and genres of repertoire for different grade levels from a variety of cultural origins and musical traditions that could serve as examples for teaching musical concepts.

What the Test Scorers Are Looking For

Even if you feel confident about your knowledge of the content to be tested, you still may wonder how you will be able to tell what the test scorers want.

In fact, the *Music: Concepts and Processes* test questions are crafted to be as clear as possible regarding what tasks you are expected to do. No expectations are hidden in the question or expressed in code words. The music educators that ETS hires to score your responses base your score on two considerations:

- Whether you do the tasks that the question asks for
- How well you do them

So, to answer more specifically the question "What do the scorers want?" we should look at two things:

- A test question—much like one you will encounter in the test
- The general scoring guide that the music educators who score your test responses follow

A sample test question

Briefly describe an instructional sequence that would introduce the concept of texture to students in a *general music* class.

In the space provided in your test book, respond to the following THREE tasks.

Task I: Indicate the grade or grade range for which your instructional sequence is intended.

Task II: Briefly describe an appropriate and logical instructional sequence for the grade level you have indicated that would introduce the concept of texture to students in a general music class. Your instructional sequence should include:

- ONE or more participatory experiences and
- TWO musical selections. The musical selections you include should come from different cultural origins or musical traditions.

You may structure the sequence in any manner you prefer—it may, for example, be for a single class period or it may occur over a span of several class periods.

Task III: Briefly describe an additional activity that reinforces what you taught about texture in Task II.

This kind of question usually appears as Question 2 in a *Music: Concepts and Processes* test.

The first thing you should notice is the "set-up" sentence in the beginning. It tells you in general terms what your response should address:

- The particular musical concept you'll teach
- The teaching goal, which is to introduce the concept to students
- The setting, a general music class

Since the question asks you to set up general music class instruction, you should not describe a rehearsal or an individual lesson. If you do, you will lose points. If you describe the concept using only university-level terms but don't describe how you would teach it to K–12 students, you'll lose points. If you go on at length about counterpoint or timbre but forget to talk about texture, you'll lose points.

Focus on the question. Let the text of the question help you focus.

Next you'll see—clearly set off in the structure of the question—the THREE major tasks you are to perform in your response. If you look at the response space in the practice test (later in this study guide), you'll see that each task fits into a pre-formatted outline. You don't, therefore, need to worry about responding in a particular style or format. Instead, focus your efforts on responding to the tasks.

Task I is very simple and is, in part, intended to help you "ease into" your response. Simply choose the grade or grade range of students you prefer to teach. If you choose a sensible range (e.g., K–1, 6–8, middle school, grade 11) it will help the scorers understand your response better. Avoid choosing a range that is too broad, such as K–12 or 2–8, since it would be difficult to describe an instructional sequence that would be equally appropriate for the youngest and oldest students in such a broad range.

Task II is the main part of the question. Notice that it asks for "an instructional sequence" that is

- logical
- appropriate

Let's consider what these two points mean.

A ***logical*** instructional sequence uses two or more activities to advance student understanding of a concept. Good instruction comes in many styles, and the scorers know that. The activities might be distinct, they might flow together seamlessly, or they might even be simultaneous. The point to worry about isn't the style—the scorers aren't scoring you on the style. Instead, describe a good, logical instructional sequence. That means that the activities should build on and reinforce understanding of the concept in a progression. It also means that you need to describe your sequence clearly so that a total stranger, such as a scorer—an experienced music educator, one who may supervise dozens of new music teachers every semester—can understand it well enough to give you the maximum number of points it deserves.

A good instructional sequence, therefore,

- has the right content,
- is in the right order, and
- is in a progression that builds students' understanding of the concept.

If you describe appropriate activities, but the activities are a disconnected jumble and don't interrelate and build upon one another to create a progressive direction toward ever-greater student understanding, you won't get as many points as you could have. Or if you describe a brilliant lesson that has nothing at all to do with the concept the question asked you to teach, you will lose quite a few points.

An ***appropriate*** sequence

- addresses the concept—that is, it is appropriate insofar as it relates to the concept,
- uses instructional methods that are proper for the grade level of the students you are teaching, and
- evinces a clear connection between the activities students will perform and how they will gain understanding of the concept.

These points will be discussed in greater detail below. For now, remember that if, for example, you are supposed to be teaching about texture but have instructional activities that address only pitch, you will lose points. Similarly, if you try to introduce first graders to polyphony by using the last movement of Ives' Fourth Symphony, you may lose points. If you describe an ill-defined or unfocused activity and assert that "from this the students will learn texture," you will lose points.

Notice that two bullets in the question specify what to include in your Task II sequence. If you don't include them, or if you don't respond adequately, you'll get fewer points. They mean exactly what they say:

- include ONE participatory activity
- and TWO musical selections.

You may include as many participatory activities as you like, but you must have at least ONE. Such an activity is one in which the students are involved in a task or action as opposed to listening to you lecture while they sit silently in their seats.

As for the musical selections, you can name specific songs or pieces, or describe a general repertoire. If you describe a general repertoire, it's advisable to clarify the connection to the concept you are teaching—for example, you might write, "Many New England fuguing tunes have a mixture of polyphony and homophony." *Any kind of music is acceptable*—for example, you might write, "Certain kinds of music of other traditions (Chinese, Arab, Turkish) employ heterophony."

Like the sequence activities themselves, the selections should ideally

- clearly exemplify the concept you are addressing, and
- be accessible to students at the grade level of the students you are teaching.

Of the two, exemplifying the concept is the more important. The point is not to produce a long list of musical selections, but rather that every selection you do list should be a clear example of the concept that is at the heart of the instructional sequence (in the sample question above, the concept is texture).

The scorers are trained specifically to give you the benefit of the doubt when they judge the grade-level appropriateness of your musical selections. They realize that your selections have been chosen on short notice in a stressful environment, and that a selection that seems a bit too childish or sophisticated to one person might work well in a classroom with the right presentation given by another person. If your selection, however, is wildly over the heads of the grade level you have chosen (e.g., Ives' Fourth Symphony for first graders, as mentioned previously), it may bring your score down.

You don't need to mention *more* than two selections, but the selections need to be significantly different culturally or stylistically. It's best if they are *very* different. The selections can, for example, come from different countries, or from different periods or traditions within the same country. For example, the fugue from the first movement of Carl Nielsen's Third Symphony and a Beatles tune like "Yellow Submarine" would provide your sequence with considerable diversity. A New England fuguing tune and a Count Basie standard are both from the United States, but their performance traditions differ enough to provide the sequence with variety. A Brahms piano concerto together with a Schumann piano concerto, or a Beatles song together with a Rolling Stones song, offer virtually no discernable variety.

The issue of musical selections has been treated at some length here—even though it is a *relatively minor part of the question*—because some test takers tend to be disproportionately concerned with the selections. The main task of the question, however, is exactly the main thing the scorers are looking for: an appropriate and logical instructional sequence for the grade level you have indicated. Don't spend all your time on selections and neglect to answer the main part of the question. The selections are not the most critical component of your score.

This is a "constructed-response" question—meaning that you must write out a response, but it doesn't have to be an essay. The note that appears at the bottom of Task II reminds you that you have the right to respond to the question in your own way. The scorers will read through your response and work to find every point you deserve. Remember, though, that it is also your responsibility, as well as to your great advantage, to respond as clearly as possible so that it is easy for the scorers to find your points.

Task III asks for an additional activity. It is left open to the test taker. It could be

- an extension or reinforcement of the previous instruction,
- an assignment,
- an assessment, or
- any other appropriate activity

It is designed to see whether you know what a reasonable additional activity might be. Whatever you choose to describe, be sure to include enough information to make it clear to the scorers that the activity relates to what you taught in Task II. Notice that the wording used for Task III reminds you to relate the additional activity in such a way.

At this point, it should be emphasized that this test is designed to assess whether you have **received**, **understood**, and **retained** the minimal training (or its equivalent) your state expects you to have so that you may begin a career as a professional music educator, in accordance with that state's standards. It is not a test of following directions. If you correctly and thoroughly answered all parts of the question, but wrote your participatory activity in the space for Task III instead of the space for Task II, would you lose points? No—you would receive full credit because you performed all the required tasks correctly. The scorers are trained to give you any reasonable benefit of the doubt. They are, furthermore, carefully supervised to ensure that they are giving appropriate scores. They do not score in an arbitrary or punishing manner. Keep in mind, though, that any departure from the text of the questions or directions is, by its very nature, risky. This will be discussed further on in this chapter.

The structure of the question is designed specifically to make it easy for you to see what the scorers want you to do. The General Scoring Guide emphasizes to scorers what they should look for.

The General Scoring Guide

Your response is scored by at least two experienced professional educators, and many of the scores are checked by a third person—the "chief scorer"—to ensure that the scores are appropriate and in accordance with the scoring guides and procedures. The two scores are added together to give you the total score for your response to the question. So if two scorers gave you 5s, your score would be 10.

Let's look at the description of the top score your response can get from a single scorer.

A score of 5

- demonstrates **full** understanding of the musical concepts and processes presented by the question
- presents musical concepts and strategies for skill development in a sequence that is **pedagogically sound**
- **correctly and thoroughly** answers all parts of the question
- uses a sufficient number of examples, all of which are **appropriate for the age or grade level** cited and are **representative of a variety of cultural origins and musical traditions**
- uses **all** musical terms accurately and spells them correctly

The underlined words are the scored elements (what the scorers are looking at) of your response. The **bold** words are the **quantitative/qualitative** aspects of the scorers' diagnosis—did you do what was asked and, if so, how well did you do it? Neither of these has anything to do with whether or not they agree with your approach, like your approach, or would teach it that way themselves. If what you do is complete, correct, and doable (within reasonable doubt allowed in your favor), you will get a 5.

If you look at each score point from 5 through 0, the elements are the same, but the **quantitative/qualitative** assessment is different. Looking, as an example, at the first element of each score point description (see General Scoring Guide in chapter 7), you can see words such as the following:

- **full**—if everything is there, correct, and appropriate, you earn a score of 5
- **substantial**—if there is a single (but not a critical) omission or an important point is a little unclear, but otherwise the response is very strong, you earn a score of 4
- **basic**—if there are some errors or omissions, but the approach will "do no harm," you earn a score of 3
- **limited**—if there are critical errors and omissions, but some understanding is apparent, you earn a score of 2
- **little or no**—if there are only tangential or remote relationships to concepts or tasks in the question, you earn a score of 1
- **no**—if nothing is correct, or nothing in the response is even tangentially related to the concepts or tasks in the question (which rarely happens), you earn a score of 0.

The topics for Question 1 in the *Concepts and Processes* test reflect common, every-day challenges you are likely to face when running rehearsals or teaching an individual lesson. In question 1, you have a choice of topic A (instrumental) or B (vocal). (For an instrumental topic, any one of the standard instrument types—strings, percussion, brass, woodwinds—may appear on any given test. Questions asking you to deal with individual instruments will typically give you a choice of instruments in the same family. Questions focusing on ensemble problems will offer you a choice of ensembles—usually band, orchestra, or jazz ensemble. Always choose the one with which you are most comfortable.)

Question 2 topics reflect the basic concepts in music we hear every day, such as rhythm, meter, pitch, form, texture, dynamics, and so on. The music field is full of basic topics that need to be taught to K-12 students. These are the topics that you will teach to those students who don't study an instrument or participate in an ensemble. They will rely on you to introduce them to basic knowledge and skills in music.

Setting Priorities When Taking the Examination

It's the day of the test. You've found a seat and you're feeling a bit nervous. A lot can come up on the test, and there are some really wild stories out there about the questions. On the other hand, you as if you know your subject, and you know how the test works because you have read the materials about it in advance. They hand out the books and warn you not to break the seal until you are told to do so. The test is about to begin.

In an ideal situation, you would open the test book and see a question based on one of your favorite topics, perhaps one you recently taught. The ideas for each of the tasks would flow effortlessly onto the page in a progressive sequence. You would have plenty of time and energy to respond to all the tasks. Your knowledge of each facet of the topic would be complete and flawless. You'd be in perfect health. You'd be just nervous enough to motivate you to do well. The room would be quiet, pleasantly appointed, and smell like an herb garden.

But what should you do if this is *not* the case? What if

- you're not all that solid on the topic?
- you feel as if you're coming down with the flu?
- you can't think of any specific examples?
- there's an annoying rumbling noise in the ventilation system?
- you're too nervous and having a hard time focusing?

In these less-than-ideal circumstances, you'll need to set and concentrate on priorities. You'll need to move methodically through the question so that you can do your best on the most important tasks. After all, no state requires a perfect score to be granted a license.

How should you do this? None of the topics in the *Concepts and Processes* test is obscure; and if you are properly trained in music and music education, you will be at least somewhat familiar with each of them. To do your best, concentrate on the following pointers.

1. Remain calm, positive, mature, and professional.
2. Identify important parts of the question. Concentrate on those first.
3. Stay with the topic. Start with what you know and build from there.
4. Keep it simple.

Think "RISK" and remember the underlined words. Saying them under your breath may even help you concentrate.

Let's look again at the sample question and use it to illustrate the pointers above.

Remain calm . . .

The topic of the question is texture. According to the *New Harvard Dictionary of Music*, texture is the "general pattern of sound created by the elements of a work or passage. For example . . . a work that is perceived as consisting of the combination of several melodic lines is said to be contrapuntal or polyphonic." Did you know and remember something like that when you saw the word "texture"? If not, you'll have to start with what you can remember about texture. By remaining calm, positive, mature, and professional, you place yourself in the best frame of mind to focus and to remember important aspects of the topic as best you can.

- Focus on the question. Don't pay any attention to wild rumors about the test.
- Don't waste your time getting angry with the test or the topic. When you are taking an exam, getting angry wastes time and energy you could be using to get it over with. No matter how angry you are, your state will not license you to teach until you have passed the test.
- Don't spend valuable time during the examination period writing a note or letter of protest to ETS in your test book. Your task during the test is to produce a response that will score as high as possible. If you have any questions to ask or comments to make about the test, do so afterward. The test-site supervisor can tell you where to send your comments.
- Be straightforward in your response. Don't put in sarcastic remarks. It's unprofessional and it wastes your time and energy. And although the scorers are trained to disregard such remarks, such behavior increases the risk of putting incorrect or inappropriate elements into your sequence. These could lower your score.

Identify important parts . . .

The question's first sentence says "describe an instructional sequence." This is the main task you will be scored on. Concentrate on the sequence first, making sure the topic is clearly explained. Next, formulate and clearly describe a good follow-up activity for Task III. Worry about musical examples later and spelling musical terms last. You have only an hour to answer both questions, so use it wisely.

- Your task is to answer the question so that the scorers can give you as many points as possible. Don't try to read their minds. Don't try to "read between the lines" and answer what you imagine the question is "really" asking. The questions are written in a straightforward and clear manner and have no hidden requirements.
- Don't waste time dwelling on subjects the question did not ask about. For example, addressing different learning styles in your sequence might help your score if you've done a good job of answering the question, but not if you write only about learning styles and fail to answer the question.
- Know when to stop writing. Give each part of the question the detail it deserves and be sure to cover all the parts, but don't waste time overresponding to less critical parts of the question. For Question 2, for example, some test takers list dozens of works from as many cultures as they can think of—then get a low score because they neglected to describe a sequence.

Stay with the topic . . .

Perhaps all you can remember about texture is that one kind uses block chords and another kind uses phenomena like canons and fugues. You may even remember (perhaps as you plan your response) that the former is called homophony and the latter polyphony. If you handle this right, you could score well. Whenever you include any secondary issues in your response (in this example, such issues might be melody, counterpoint, voice leading, tonality, etc.), be sure you relate everything back to the topic.

- Don't ramble on about related—or unrelated—topics and lose track of the topic in the question.
- Keep your answer consistent with the focus of the question. Talk about the parts of the topic you really know and stick with them. Don't try to change the focus of the question. Even if your recollection is somewhat imperfect, you can still make points as long as some of what you say is correct and applies to the assigned topic.
- Never change the topic—for example, by announcing in your opening sentence that you know nothing about texture, so you will write about the overtone series instead. You would run a serious risk of earning a score of 0. The scorers need you to answer the assigned question so that they can give you as many points as possible. If you answer a different question, they can't give you points.

Keep it simple . . .

Use a transparent, simple response style that is easy to read. The scorers suggest that *it's better to write an outline or a series of short statements or descriptions* so that you can keep track of what your sequence is teaching. That way, you can track how well you have responded to the main parts of the question. It also makes it easier for the scorers to find the good things you've done and award you points accordingly.

- You *don't* have to write an essay or waste your time on charming or clever prose. This is not an English composition test, so your writing style is not being scored. You will not get extra points for writing an essay. Use techniques that allow you to communicate information efficiently and clearly. For example, you can use a bulleted list as long as you explain and clarify how the listed materials will be used. You can also use a numbered list if you are communicating, for example, a sequence of steps you would take in response to a situation presented in the question.
- Fill as much of the response space as you need, and no more. The test form purposely gives you more space than you need, just in case. You are scored according to how correctly and thoroughly you answer the question, not by the number of words.

Examples of Responses and the Scores They Earned

Let's look at three responses to the sample question on texture and see why they got the scores they did. (The responses appear below in print rather than in their original handwritten form for easier readability.)

Sample Response that Earned a Score of 5

Task I: Grade or grade range: 9–12

Task II: Briefly describe an appropriate and logical instructional sequence (include TWO musical selections from different cultural origins or musical traditions and ONE or more participatory experiences).

1. Outline concepts you'll cover—should have it on blackboard...

   - monophonic is only a melody by itself—as in mono + phony = "single sound"
   - homophony is a melody with accompaniment ("accomp. in the background, not as featured") OR everyone does block chords ("like a chorale or church hymn"), as in same + sound
   - polyphony is all of the parts have a melody—maybe the same melody but entering at different times ("like a canon or a round, all the parts are melodic and are equally important"), as in many + sounds

2. Next, play a recording of Muslim chant. Ask them to think about what the texture might be and see if someone can guess it. Pick someone (otherwise only the assertive kids participate), ask her/him to explain it to the class. Assure the student uses the right terms as you have them on the board.

3. Next play a recording of Krystler (sp?). He arranged a lot of music for violin and piano. Ask them to think about the texture. Pick a different student this time, who can explain why it is homophonic (as on the board). You could follow up with Tori Amos, she sings some unaccomp. songs, or "O Lord, won't you buy me a color TV." That's going back to monophony again so they don't just follow your pattern on the board. Return to homophony with some Billing's ("Chester" or something else up-tempo).

4. For polyphony, play some Palestrina. Pick students as above and make them think the concepts through as shown on the board.

Task III: Briefly describe an additional activity that reinforces what you taught about texture in Task II.

1. Have them sing the "Are you Sleeping Brother" melody together. Say "we have one tune and everybody singing it—what texture is that?"

2. Sing "Are you Sleeping" with the girls singing melody and the boys singing "row" on tonic-then-on the beats. Have the boys and girls switch parts. have a melody and accompaniment—what kind texture is that?"

3. Have them sing the round in the traditional way. "What texture is that? Why?" Keep referring to what you wrote on the board for definitions so they stay consistent.

What the test taker earning a 5 has done

Test Scorers' Guidelines (Describing a response that earned a 5)	Test Taker's Response
▪ demonstrates **full** understanding of the musical concepts and processes presented by the question	The test taker's understanding of texture is excellent, and the evidence to support that conclusion is abundant. The response shows significant evidence that the test taker understands how students acquire understanding and includes details demonstrating an awareness of pitfalls that may occur in a typical instructional situation. The lesson is set in a general music class.
▪ presents musical concepts and strategies for skill development in a sequence that is **pedagogically sound**	The instructional sequence is appropriate for the age of the students. It is energetic, focused, and enthusiastic, keeping the students engaged with the materials. It builds student understanding progressively, beginning with a simple texture and contrasting it with more complex textures. During the lecture/presentation portion, the instructor helps the students reach understanding by asking them questions (the "Socratic" approach). The activity for Task III gets the students involved in creating the textures about which they are learning using a folk song with which they are likely familiar.

- **correctly and thoroughly** answers all parts of the question

All parts of the question are correctly and thoroughly answered. The extra details in the response are relevant and serve to clarify that the test taker understands the concepts and processes in the question.

- uses a sufficient number of examples, all of which are **appropriate for the age or grade level** cited and are **representative of a variety of cultural origins and musical traditions**

Although two would have been enough (that's all the question asks for), lots of examples were cited. The extra examples are simply part of the way the test taker conceived of the sequence and are in no way excessive. They were genuinely representative of a wide variety of traditions and would clearly demonstrate the various textures to students of this age.

- uses **all** musical terms accurately and spells them correctly

Since this is not an examination to test English writing skills, the use of abbreviations (e.g., "accomp." for accompaniment) is of no concern to the scorers. The musical terms are used correctly and they are spelled correctly.

What the test taker earning 5 has *not* done

- The test taker left out heterophony and monody—but this is not a significant omission. The question asks the test taker to introduce the concept of texture to a class. Covering every kind of texture, therefore, would not be necessary. Monody and heterophony, in fact, could just as well have confused students who are encountering the concept of texture for the first time.
- The test taker placed the participatory activity in Task III instead of Task II. Overall, however, the sequence is so complete and strong (even the lecture/presentation requires active participation by students) that giving it a score of 4 for a minor departure from the directions was not deemed fair to the test taker, nor did a score of 4 seem to accord with the overall quality of the response. Since the scorers are trained both to give the test taker the benefit of the doubt and to give the higher score when they are "on the line," the higher score was awarded.
- The connections between the sequence's activities and how the students will learn the concepts were somewhat indirect. Two elements included in the response, however, were sufficient to give the benefit of the doubt to the higher score:

  1. The sequence is one that shows high potential for success.
  2. Phrases such as "**assure the student uses the right terms as you have them on the board**" and "**keep referring to what you wrote on the board for definitions so they stay consistent**" indicate that the initial explanation of texture, as written on the board, will be used to underpin such connections as necessary.

Overall assessment of performance

The scorers know that the test taker has only a half hour to quickly address the many tasks in the question. This response thoroughly addresses, as a whole, the critical aspect of the question ("Briefly describe an appropriate and logical instructional sequence . . .").

Sample Response that Earned a Score of 3

Task I: Grade or grade range: 9–12

Task II: Briefly describe an appropriate and logical instructional sequence (include TWO musical selections from different cultural origins or musical traditions and ONE or more participatory experiences).

1. Discuss the idea of single melodic line. Play a recording of Gregorian chant or plainsong. Discuss origin and time period of monophonic music. Students could participate in singing in unison some melodic line.

2. Next cover polyphony. Examples of Medieval and Renaissance music could be played and discussed. The students could then sing a round.

3. Homophony should be covered next. Bach chorales could be played. Participation would be limited to the vocal abilities of the class. Perhaps a sustained chord could be held to give more understanding of homophonic texture. Explain the difference between polyphony and homophony.

The class should be broken up into smaller times for listening, lecture, discussion and activity.

Task III: Briefly describe an additional activity that reinforces what you taught about texture in Task II.

High school students might not be ready to go beyond these forms. Some selections of polytonalities could be played to give students an idea of the range of possibilities for texture in music.

Have them find an example for the next class period of each kind of texture. They could play the CDs they found and explain what kind of music it is, what kind of texture it is, and what they like about the music's texture.

What the test taker earning 3 has done

Test Scorers' Guidelines (Describing a response that earned a 3)	Test Taker's Response
▪ demonstrates basic understanding of the musical concepts and processes presented by the question	The test taker's understanding of texture is basically correct. Some mistakes, however, regarding texture are present. The lesson is set in a general music class.
▪ presents musical concepts and strategies for skill development in a **sequence** that is in part pedagogically sound	The response is a vague description of some more-or-less appropriate activities that are thrust forward with the hope the students will somehow acquire understanding of the concept. Although bringing historical perspectives into instruction on texture is laudable, it serves in this case to obscure the progression of the lesson.
▪ provides **basically correct** answers to the major parts of the question	Major parts of the question are addressed, although vaguely, perfunctorily, and, in some cases, with misleading content.
▪ uses some examples, most of which are **appropriate for the age or grade level** cited and are **representative of a variety of cultural origins and musical traditions**	Gregorian chant and Bach chorales provide some, though not strong, contrast in musical traditions.
▪ uses **most** musical terms accurately and spells most of them correctly	The musical terms are spelled correctly but are sometimes used incorrectly.

What the test taker earning 3 has *not* done

- The exercise in part 3 of Task II ("**a sustained chord could be held...**") is not an appropriate example of homophony and could mislead the students. Polytonality is not a texture. It would have been better to describe briefly how homophony and polyphony differ (Task II, part 3).
- The response shows little evidence that the test taker understands how students acquire understanding. Although participatory elements are introduced into the sequence, they are vaguely defined, and there is no indication of how the activity will be used by either the teacher or the student to advance or reinforce understanding of the concept. The statement "**The class should be broken up into smaller times for listening, lecture, discussion and activity**" does not illuminate the test taker's understanding of instruction.
- Task III begins ominously, then turns toward a more-or-less appropriate activity that needs more supporting instruction, structure, and definition if it is to be pedagogically viable.
- The instructional sequence is predicated on low expectations of what the students can accomplish. It is lethargic, unfocused, and unenthusiastic. For the most part, the teacher talks while the students listen.

Overall assessment of performance

This response provides, as a whole, basically correct responses to most parts of the question.

Sample Response that Earned a Score of 1

Task I: Grade or grade range: 6–8

Task II: Briefly describe an appropriate and logical instructional sequence (include TWO musical selections from different cultural origins or musical traditions and ONE or more participatory experiences).

Address each domain.

Psychomotor

Affective

Cognitive

Begin by saying "we're going to learn about texture."

Write the word texture on the board. Ask them about textures that are rough, smooth, thick and thin that they can find around the house or at school.

Have them make 10 color paper labels labeled "thick" and "thin" etc. and have them label things in the room with them. This participatory experience will address the cognitive domain.

Ask them how they feel when they touch something smooth. Play some smooth music like a Bach chorale and hear how smooth it is and soothing. Then ask them how rough feels and play "Ride of the Valkyries." These would address the affective domain. They could then pretend they are having a rough ride and gallop around the room. This would address the psychomotor domain while emphasizing rough texture.

Task III: Briefly describe an additional activity that reinforces what you taught about texture in Task II.

Play CDs of different music –

Beethoven 3rd Sym., Perotin organum, Shubert "Death and the Maiden," West African finger piano, Sousa marches, Charlie Parker, Bruckner "Te deum," Kabelevsky piano music, Arvo Part "Miserere," Carter "Concerto for Orchestra," Bartok 2nd piano concerto, the Chieftains, etc. Have the students hold up their labels when the music is thin, thick, etc. Give a test. Play more music and have the students write down the textures. Collect these and score them.

What the test taker earning 1 has done

Test Scorers' Guidelines (Describing a response that earned a 1)	Test Taker's Response
▪ demonstrates **little or no** understanding of the musical concepts and processes presented by the question	The intention to address cognitive domains is commendable, and the setting is clearly that of a general music class. The understanding of texture, however, is colloquial rather than musical.
▪ does **not answer any** part of the question correctly but **provides some ideas that relate** to the question	There is an attempt to create an assessment activity in Task III.
▪ does **not** present musical concepts and strategies for skill development in a sequence that is pedagogically sound	Activities at this developmental level of understanding might make sense for K-1 students, but they are too infantile for 6-8 students. There is no discernable progression in the sequence.
▪ uses **no** examples that are appropriate for the age or grade level cited or are representative of a variety of cultural origins and musical traditions	While it can be said that many Protestant chorales are "smooth" compared to the Wagner example, the conception of "texture" in this sequence is predicated on the subjective notions of the test taker. Bach and Wagner examples provide little cultural variety, and the lengthy list in Task III does not illuminate the test taker's understanding of texture or instructional practice.
▪ does **not** use musical terms accurately or spell them correctly	Virtually no musical terms are used at all because the response does not discuss a musical aspect of the examples.

What the test taker earning 1 has *not* done

- Although the test taker has provided some ideas that relate very tangentially to the question, he or she has failed to respond appropriately to any part. This is partly because the conception of texture was incorrect, partly because the activities were infantile for the grade level chosen, and partly because the response was more preoccupied with addressing cognitive domains than teaching the concept in a progressive sequence.

Overall assessment of performance

This response is characterized in too many places by little or no understanding of the musical or instructional concepts and processes presented in the question.

Notes on Responding to Questions 1A and 1B

The general scoring guidelines are designed to accommodate all question types that might appear on the test. A description of an extended instructional sequence is the main task in the general music class question 2. That question also asks for musical examples from a variety of origins.

Questions 1A and 1B, on the other hand, as you will see in the practice test, often do not ask for musical examples. Parts of these questions involve sequence only in a limited way. If such components are not in the question, you won't be scored on them, so you don't need to add them. Concern yourself only with what a question asks for, and do not assume that all questions demand the same kinds of responses.

Conclusion

Now you are ready to take the practice test in chapter 9. Practice your skills in analyzing the question, planning your response, and writing your response based on your notes. In chapter 10 you will find sample responses to the practice test. You can compare your answers to those samples and gauge your performance based on the scores the sample received and the comments made by the expert scorer.

Chapter 9

Practice Test, *Music: Concepts and Processes*

► ► ► ► ► ► ► ► ► ► ► ►

Now that you have studied the topics and have worked through strategies relating to answering and scoring constructed-response questions, you can try the following practice test. You might find it helpful to simulate actual testing conditions, giving yourself 60 minutes to work on the questions. If you make a photocopy of the practice test, you can have a clean copy to write on each time you try the test.

When you have finished the practice test, you can compare your responses to the sample responses in the following chapters. In those chapters, each sample response is followed by analytical remarks provided by one of the test's chief scorers.

Keep in mind that the questions on the test you take at an actual administration will be based on different topics, although the tasks in each question will be approximately the same.

THE **PRAXIS**
S E R I E S
Professional Assessments for Beginning Teachers ®

TEST NAME:

Music: Concepts and Processes Practice Test

Time—60 Minutes

2 Questions

Question 1
(Suggested time—30 minutes)

Choose ONE of the two topics below and respond to it in the appropriate space in this test book. Indicate your choice of topic by circling A or B at the top of page 119.

TOPIC A: INSTRUMENTAL

- Choose ONE of the following woodwind instruments.
  Flute
  Oboe
  B-flat clarinet
  Bassoon
  Alto saxophone
- For the instrument you have chosen, identify and briefly describe THREE possible causes of poor tone quality. Choose a specific instrument and write your choice in the space provided on page 119.
- Briefly describe ONE specific remedial technique that can be used to correct each of the problems you identify.

TOPIC B: CHORAL

A beginning high school choir is flatting (tending to go flat) in a chromatic section of an a cappella piece that lies in a high tessitura for all voices. The singers have learned the notes correctly, but the flatting persists.

- Identify and briefly describe THREE possible causes of this flatting.
- Briefly describe ONE specific remedial technique that can be used to correct each of the problems you identify.

RESPOND TO QUESTION 1 HERE
(Note: You are not required to fill all of the space provided.)

Circle your chosen topic: TOPIC A (specify instrument: ________________) TOPIC B

Cause 1:

Remedial Technique for Cause 1:

CONTINUE TO RESPOND TO QUESTION 1 HERE
(Note: You are not required to fill all of the space provided.)

Cause 2:

Remedial Technique for Cause 2:

CONTINUE TO RESPOND TO QUESTION 1 HERE
(Note: You are not required to fill all of the space provided.)

Cause 3:

Remedial Technique for Cause 3:

Question 2
(Suggested time—30 minutes)

Briefly describe an instructional sequence that would teach major and minor modes (tonalities) to students in a general music class.

In the space provided in your test book, respond to the following THREE tasks.

Task I: At the top of page 123, indicate the grade or grade range for which your instructional sequence is intended.

Task II: On pages 123 and 124, briefly describe an appropriate and logical instructional sequence for the grade level you have indicated that would teach major and minor modes to students in a general music class. Your instructional sequence should include

- ONE or more participatory experiences andc
- TWO musical selections. The musical selections you include should come from different cultural origins or musical traditions.

You may structure the sequence in any manner you prefer—it may, for example, be for a single class period or it may occur over a span of several class periods.

Task III: On page 133, briefly describe an additional activity that reinforces what you taught about major and minor modes in Task II.

RESPOND TO QUESTION 2 HERE
(Note: You are not required to fill all of the space provided.)

Task I: Grade or grade range: ____________

Task II: Briefly describe an appropriate and logical instructional sequence (include TWO musical selections from different cultural origins or musical traditions and ONE or more participatory experiences).

CONTINUE TO RESPOND TO QUESTION 2 HERE
(Note: You are not required to fill all of the space provided.)

Task II (instructional sequence), continued:

CONTINUE TO RESPOND TO QUESTION 2 HERE
(Note: You are not required to fill all of the space provided.)

Task III: Briefly describe an additional activity that reinforces what you taught about major and minor modes

Chapter 10

Sample Responses to Question 1A of *Music: Concepts and Processes* and How They Were Scored

► ► ► ► ► ► ► ► ► ► ► ►

Music: Concepts and Processes

Question 1, TOPIC A: INSTRUMENTAL

This question tests your ability to analyze a musical problem, determine three causes, and provide possible solutions that demonstrate your knowledge of instrumental teaching, tone (timbre) production, instrumental techniques, and teaching strategies.

Study the following sample responses and commentary by scorers. Note that the responses by test takers are transcribed as the test takers wrote them, with misspellings and grammar problems uncorrected. Scorers do not assess test takers' writing skills.

Sample Response that Earned a Score of 5

RESPOND TO QUESTION 1 HERE
(Note: You are not required to fill all of the space provided.)

Circle your chosen topic: TOPIC A (specify instrument: B♭ Clarinet) TOPIC B

Cause 1:

The student playing clarinet may not be fully covering the holes for a specific note or multiple notes.

Remedial Technique for Cause 1:

A quick remedy to help students learn to properly cover the tone holes on clarinet is to have the students cover the holes on a specific note and hold them in place. This should be an easy note for the student to play, one that they are not usually having trouble performing. You should check to be certain that they are fully covering the tone holes. Then, instruct the student to play the note and then quickly look at their fingertips. When they lift up their fingers they should see an indention near their fingertips where their fingers were covering the holes. This process allows you as the teacher to check your students, and also allows you students a method of checking themselves both inside and outside of class.

Scoring Commentary

Cause 1: The test taker correctly identifies a possible cause of poor tone quality.

Remedial Technique for Cause 1: The test taker demonstrates the ability to sequence learning appropriately by describing a strategy that begins on a level the students are familiar and comfortable with, "an easy note for the students to play." The strategy presents the concept of correct finger placement to the students and allows them to practice correctly on their own, as the test taker indicates.

Cause 2:

The student may not be using proper breath support.

Remedial Technique for Cause 2:

A clarinettist who is not using proper breath support typically is not putting the right type of air into the instrument. Make sure that the student is breathing correctly by first correcting improper posture. When the student is sitting up straight with both feet on the floor, have the student take in a full, deep breath without his or her shoulders raising up or his or her body otherwise becoming tense. Tell the clarinettist that he or she should put very warm "dark" air into the instrument and that his or her tone will become just like the air they put into the horn. However, avoid letting the clarinettist overblow, especially when they are "crossing the break" (between B^b and B) or they will produce a very loud, crass sound. Instruct instead towards a constant, full breath support across all dynamic ranges.

Scoring Commentary

Cause 2: The test taker correctly identifies a second possible cause of poor tone quality.

Remedial Technique for Cause 2: The first statement, a reference to the "right type of air," is confusing, but the test taker's elaboration clarifies the meaning. By beginning with a reference to proper posture, the test taker demonstrates the ability to sequence learning. The directions include the basics of good breathing: posture, deep breathing, and a lack of tension. The caution against overblowing and the attention to the necessity of constant full breath support demonstrate a comprehensive understanding of the processes involved. The response's score was not brought down because of the misspelling ("clarinettist")—since "clarinetist" is not strictly speaking a musical term (on the same technical level as chalumeau, allegro, embouchure, passacaglia, etc.), the test taker was given the benefit of the doubt.

Cause 3:

The clarinetist may not be using the correct embouchure.

Remedial Technique for Cause 3:

The remedial technique for this problem is to check to see that the student is not taking too much or too little mouth piece into the mouth. Typically approximated 1/3 of the mouth piece playing area should be taken in. Remind the student of how the teeth and bottom lip should be placed, and that the student should think about keeping the proper amount of tightness around the entire mouth piece. Have the student demonstrate this skill multiple times and instruct them while looking into a mirror so they can see what their embouchure looks like when shaped correctly. This is an activity which they can practice when not at school. Also, have the student correctly play a note and then have him or her describe how it felt in their embouchure.

Scoring Commentary

Cause 3: The test taker correctly identifies a third possible cause of poor tone quality.

Remedial Technique for Cause 3: The test taker describes an appropriate instructional technique. While more details could be given, such as the exact position of the bottom lip over the teeth, the test taker addresses the key points of establishing a correct embouchure.

After describing correct embouchure, the test taker suggests several remedial techniques that address the needs of aural, visual, and kinesthetic learners.

This response demonstrates a full understanding of the musical concepts and processes involved and receives a score of 5.

Sample Response that Earned a Score of 4

RESPOND TO QUESTION 1 HERE
(Note: You are not required to fill all of the space provided.)

Circle your chosen topic: (TOPIC A (specify instrument B^{b} Clarinet)) TOPIC B

Cause 1:

One possible cause could be from poor breath support. Breathing correctly is essential in producing a good sound on the B^{b} clarinet. Lack of breath support effects both tone quality and intonation.

Remedial Technique for Cause 1:

The first thing to look for is good posture. The student should be sitting up straight with their back off of the back of the chair. Head should be straight, making certain to not tilt to one side. A technique to use in achieving good breath support is to make sure they are breathing from their diaphragm. You can have the student lay flat on the floor and place a book on their stomach. The goal is to make the book raise when they inhale. You can also work on long tones to listen for changes in pitch. Reassure that the students blows "through the horn", not at it. You can also have the student take a piece of paper, hold it flat against a wall and begin blowing air. Let go of other paper and your breath should keep it against the wall.

Scoring Commentary

Cause 1: The test taker correctly identifies poor breath support as a cause of poor tone quality.

Remedial Technique for Cause 1: The test taker develops the concept of proper breath support by first describing good posture. Unfortunately, the concept of proper breath support is not explained as well. Students should be told more about breath support than just to breathe from the diaphragm. Because the test taker discusses three techniques that help to demonstrate and practice breath support, he or she does receive partial credit.

Cause 2:

Another cause of poor tone quality on the clarinet is in their embouchure. A clarinet player's embouchure should be a flat chin and tight corners of their mouth.

Remedial Technique for Cause 2:

One technique helpful for this problem is to play in front of a mirror. A mirror allows the player to see that his/her chin is not as tight and flat as it should be. The player can also look and see if the corners of their mouths are tight. The bottom lip should also cover the bottom teeth, and a mirror will allow the student to check this area. One thing the director can do is try to move the clarinet while the student is playing. If the student has the correct embouchure setting, the clarinet will not wiggle from side to side.

Scoring Commentary

Cause 2: The test taker correctly identifies a second cause.

Remedial Technique for Cause 2: The correct embouchure is presented, but the test taker's response should also include a description of how much of the mouthpiece should be in the mouth. The last suggestion weakens the response, and should be omitted: moving an instrument in the student's mouth while the student is playing can cause injury.

Cause 3:

The third cause of poor tone quality could be in the reed. The strongness/weakness of the reed aids in tone quality. The brand and overall shape of the reed affects tone quality as well.

Remedial Technique for Cause 3:

A technique would be to inform the students what reeds are good/bad. Some brands are okay for beginners, but reeds are available that are more suitable for students as they progress. The size of the reed should also be addressed to students. Beginners should start off on a 1 1/2 or 2 size reed. As students progress, reeds should increase in size. The ideal goal would be to play on a 2 1/2 or even size 4 clarinet reed.

Also, teach students to remove the reed after playing and store it in a reed case or some type of protector. Students should also be taught to check for chips in the reed or to identify if the reed is warped.

Scoring Commentary

Cause 3: The test taker correctly identifies a third cause of poor tone quality.

Remedial Technique for Cause 3: The response shows a substantial knowledge of reeds. However, more specificity regarding when and why to increase a student's reed strength could have improved the response. The additional instruction about storing the reed in a reed case and checking for cracks or chips is appropriate, although other common methods of protecting the reed, such as using the mouthpiece cap whenever the instrument is not being played, could be stressed. The test taker could also instruct the student to wet the reed before placing it on the mouthpiece.

Overall, this response demonstrates a substantial understanding of the musical concepts and processes and receives a score of 4.

Sample Response that Earned a Score of 3

RESPOND TO QUESTION 1 HERE
(Note: You are not required to fill all of the space provided.)

Circle your chosen topic: (TOPIC A (specify instrument: B♭ clarinet)) TOPIC B

Cause 1:

Weak embouchure to support note(s) being played.

Remedial Technique for Cause 1:

I would begin by having the student play a specified note within the middle range of the instrument. I would have them hold that note for approximately ten seconds without wavering. Then I would have the student tighten up the lower lip against the teeth. I would have the student use their hand to feel the difference between how the lip felt before and how it feels when tightened. The student would then try playing the same note again with the embouchure tightened and instruct them to listen to the difference. Finally, I would have the student play a C Major scale keeping the lip in the same position to reinforce the positioning. The student will have to be reminded occasionally of this tip.

Scoring Commentary

Cause 1: The test taker correctly identifies a cause of poor tone quality.

Remedial Technique for Cause 1: The response provides evidence of only a basic understanding of a teaching strategy that would improve embouchure. The response describes improving embouchure only by the suggestion to the students to "tighten up the lower lip against the teeth." Other important aspects are not mentioned—e.g., how much of the mouthpiece to put into the mouth, the position of the mouth and upper lips, or the importance of sealing the lips around the mouthpiece and tightening the corners of the mouth.

Failing to address these aspects weakens the response. The remedial technique of comparing the sensation and sound of playing with and without incorrect embouchure is appropriate, but only after the students understand all that correct embouchure entails.

Beginning with a single note and advancing to a C major scale would be rather a drastic sequential step, but it indicates that the test taker is aware of the necessity of beginning with simple skills before advancing to more difficult skills. A better sequence would be to advance from a single note to a series of a few notes, gradually working up to playing a scale.

Cause 2:

breathing technique

Remedial Technique for Cause 2:

I would have the student take in air and try sustaining a note for a period of about 10 seconds. Next, without using the instrument I would have the student sit tall in chair place hands around waist and breath in slowly to fill up "tire around the waist." We would also practice letting that air out slowly with instrument we would take in the air in the same way and let it out slowly while sustaining the specified note. We would then try it using a scale, in one breath ascending & one breath descending using different note values, until the student understands that a constant flow of air improves the tone quality of the instrument.

Scoring Commentary

Cause 2: The test taker identifies an "error in breathing technique" as a cause of poor tone quality but does not describe a specific error such as a lack of breath support or overblowing. Because the test taker uses a vague term without elaboration or examples, it is unclear how well the test taker understands the musical concept and processes involved.

Remedial Technique for Cause 2: The test taker instructs the student to sit tall and breathe deeply, and provides an appropriate image of filling up a "tire around the waist." This is a good start, but the response suffers from a lack of specific details about this technique. Students need more direction than "letting that air out slowly" to understand and practice breath support. The test taker should include instruction on an even, steady exhalation by suggesting a steady stream of air. Alternatively, the test taker could continue with the imagery of the tire and describe the exhalation as a slow, steady leak and have students practice "hissing" out the air for a designated number of beats. The sequence of applying this breathing technique to a major scale, immediately following a single note, would be better if students were asked to include a series of a few notes in a single breath and eventually were asked to include an entire scale.

Just playing the scale "using different note values until the student understands" is a poor teaching strategy. The sequence of the response should be reversed. The students should first understand that a constant flow of air improves tone quality with a single note. The students will not be able to realize good tone unless the breath is controlled. Practicing scales with different note values does not develop this understanding. Scales should be practiced to strengthen the breath support rather than to teach breath support. Proper breath support must be introduced first.

The test taker uses a strategy and sequence that are almost identical to remedial technique 1, merely replacing the concept of embouchure with the concept of breathing technique. The response also, unfortunately, uses the same framework of playing a single note then advancing to a scale for two of the three solutions. Describing a different approach for each remedial technique would provide evidence that the test taker is aware of various strategies and would strengthen the response. By using the same routine, however, the test taker demonstrates limited teaching strategies and ideas.

Cause 3:

Saliva in instrument creating a raspy tone.

Remedial Technique for Cause 3:

I would explain to the student that an amount of saliva naturally ends up inside the instrument when it is played. I would show the student how the instrument needs to be cleaned following every use with a swab cloth (and sometimes during a rehearsal) depending on the student. I would also check to make sure that the student has rinsed out their mouth before playing the instrument and is not eating or chewing gum that might end up inside the instrument affecting the quality as well.

Scoring Commentary

Cause 3: The test taker correctly identifies a cause of poor tone quality.

Remedial Technique for Cause 3: The response begins by appropriately addressing instrumental care and guidelines for playing instruments, including no chewing gum and no eating.

Because this response indicates, overall, a basic understanding of the music concepts and processes involved, it receives a score of 3.

Sample Response that Earned a Score of 2

RESPOND TO QUESTION 1 HERE
(Note: You are not required to fill all of the space provided.)

Circle your chosen topic: (TOPIC A (specify instrument: B-flat clarinet)) TOPIC B

Cause 1:

The key hole is not completely covered.

Remedial Technique for Cause 1:

I want to describe about technique that we can use to correct each of the problems that I identify. First, in order to make sure to cover the key hole completely, we need to see our finger palm after we cover the holes. If we can see the circles in all of our finger palms we covered well. And also try to cover HARD so that we can have deep circle prints in our fingers.

Scoring Commentary

Cause 1: The test taker has correctly identified a cause of poor tone quality but should articulate this more appropriately. A correct finger position should cover all holes (not just one key hole) completely.

Remedial Technique for Cause 1: The first sentence is irrelevant and could be omitted entirely. The remedial technique is acceptable, but the last statement causes concern. Covering the holes "hard" may produce tension in the fingers, wrists, and arms that would impede technical development and agility. This statement weakens the response.

Cause 2

We don't not firm or completely cover our lips when we blow.

Remedial Technique for Cause 2:

In order to close lips and make sure it is closed right as we blow, take just the mouthpiece & blow. If we make nice sound out of just blowing mouthpiece, that means we covered our lips firmly. If not then, we have to try to covered our lips firmly until we make nice sound just by blowing mouthpiece.

Scoring Commentary

Cause 2: The description of "firming the lips or completely covering the lips" is inaccurate. The proper embouchure for the clarinet would involve lips sealed around the mouthpiece. If the test taker had provided more detail, perhaps some credit could have been given.

Remedial Technique for Cause 2: This solution is inaccurate. Blowing into the mouthpiece will produce a high pitched squeal, not a good tone. Without explanation of the proper embouchure, the test taker is advocating a trial-and-error method of remediation, a poor use of time and effort. If the correct embouchure had been explained, perhaps using only the mouthpiece could be the next step in developing a good tone.

Cause 3:

All the body parts don't fit exactly right or fit all the way in.

Remedial Technique for Cause 3:

In order to make sure all the parts are fitted all the way in, try to twist and push down all the way in & see if there are some parts that slip or slide out easily. Or if the parts are hard to push down, use cork grease to make parts slide in smoothly.

Scoring Commentary

Cause 3: This cause would affect the sound production and the tone quality, but it is described poorly.

Remedial Technique for Cause 3: The solution could have addressed the steps taken to instruct the students in proper care and assembly of the instrument. Careless twisting or pushing on parts of an assembled clarinet can have seriously negative effects on the functionality of the instrument. Specific instructions, rather than general comments, would have strengthened the response.

This response demonstrates a limited understanding of the musical concepts and processes and receives a score of 2.

Sample Response that Earned a Score of 1

RESPOND TO QUESTION 1 HERE

Circle your chosen topic: (TOPIC A (specify instrument: FLUTE)) TOPIC B

Cause 1

Over powered air flow

Remedial Technique for Cause 1:

Need output just so much air in to the instrument to make clear sound.

Scoring Commentary

Cause 1: This cause is not articulated appropriately. The test taker could have used the common musical term, "overblowing."

Remedial Technique for Cause 1: This is actually only an elaboration of the cause. It does not offer a solution. The test taker should have addressed how this would be explained to the student, and how it would be practiced.

Cause 2

Fingering mistake

Remedial Technique for Cause 2

Must use correct fingering to produce correct sound

Scoring Commentary

Cause 2: The test taker incorrectly identifies a fingering mistake as a cause of poor tone quality. This would typically result in a wrong note, not poor timbre.

Remedial Technique for Cause 2: The test taker conveys no knowledge of how to address the problem; the cause is simply restated.

Cause 3:

Wrong direction of the air flow

Remedial Technique for Cause 3

Position lips the way that air get into mouth piece, and not outside of instrument.

Scoring Commentary

Cause 3: This response is too vague to receive credit.

Remedial Technique for Cause 3: The explanation reveals that the test taker is discussing an embouchure problem, but it is too general to demonstrate the test taker's understanding of the processes involved. The test taker should have described a specific embouchure problem.

The incorrect or vague identification of causes and the lack of appropriate solutions demonstrate little or no understanding of the musical concepts and processes. This response receives a score of 1.

Chapter 11

Sample Responses to Question 1B of *Music: Concepts and Processes* and How They Were Scored

► ► ► ► ► ► ► ► ► ► ► ►

Music: Concepts and Processes

Question 1, TOPIC B: CHORAL

This question tests your ability to analyze a musical problem, determine three causes, and provide possible solutions that demonstrate your knowledge of choral rehearsal techniques, vocal production, vocal techniques, and teaching strategies.

Study the following sample responses and commentary by the scorers.

Sample Response that Earned a Score of 5

RESPOND TO QUESTION 1 HERE
(Note: You are not required to fill all of the space provided.)

Circle your chosen topic: TOPIC A (specify instrument: _______________) (TOPIC B)

Cause 1:

When singers sing in a high tessitura, they have a tendency to not alter the vowels on the top pitches. As the pitch goes up, you must open the vowels. For instance, if you are singing an "Aw" sound in the higher registers, you must open your mouth wider & sing an "Ah"

Remedial Technique for Cause 1:

- Put the music away for a while & practice singing different vowels in the higher register. start w/"Aw". Have the students sing an ugly "Aw" sound, then have them slightly alter that "Aw" to an "Ah". Check the initial pitch you gave them for the "AW" again to make sure the students are in tune. They will probably sound very flat on the "Aw" sound, but the tone quality will match on the "Ah" sound.
- Sing the chromatic section again on an "Aw" sound. As the pitches get higher, have the students alter more toward the "Ah" sound. The pitch should be in tune by this point.
- Add the words. As the pitches go higher, the jaw should drop & the mouth will open wider to compensate. The same thing happens when you change from the "Aw" to the "Ah." Check the pitches with the piano.

Scoring Commentary

Cause 1: The test taker correctly identifies the need for vowel modification and provides an appropriate example.

Remedial Technique for Cause 1: The test taker provides an appropriate sequence for correcting the problem. Beginning with only vowels, the test taker demonstrates an ability to isolate the problem and recognize the initial step in correction. Moving from individual pitches to the chromatic passage while still focusing only on the modified vowel sound is an appropriate and logical transition. The test taker completes the remedial technique by putting what has been practiced in isolated drill back into the musical passage with words. This sequence demonstrates the test taker's ability to diagnose and correct a musical problem.

Cause 2:

The students aren't opening enough in the back of the mouth. As the pitch goes up into the higher registers, the students aren't lifting their soft palette.

Remedial Technique for Cause 2:

- Once again, have the students put their music away. Have them do "yawn sighs" to practice keeping the back of the throat free & open. As they pretend to yawn, have the students speak w/the lifted soft pallate. Do the pretend yawn again & come down the scale, singing w/the lifted soft palette.

OR

- Have the students sing a nasty "E" sound with their mouths in a smiling position. Have them gradually over compensate for this bright, spread tone by pretending they have an egg in the back on their mouth. Have them explain the difference between bright tone (spread vowels) & the rounded, more resonant tone. (more space in the back of the mouth/lifted soft pallate).
- Return to the music & have the students sing the chromatic passage using the more rounded/egg in the back of the throat/"O" space sound. The pitch should be greatly improved.

Scoring Commentary

Cause 2: The test taker correctly identifies a second possible cause.

Remedial Technique for Cause 2: The test taker supplies two solutions, although either alone would have been sufficient. By returning to the music, the test taker again demonstrates how the transition from theory into practice is achieved.

Cause 3:

Bad posture - slouching causes the pitch to go flat because your ribs have to widened & opened to produce the proper amount of air to keep on pitch. Your back must be straight to keep the rib cage lifted.

Remedial Technique for Cause 3:

- Do shoulder rolls to loosen the tension in the shoulders.
- Roll the neck to loosen tension in the neck and throat.
- Roll your head from side to side to relieve tension in the neck & throat.
- Stand on your "tippy toes" & reach for the sky. As you slowly drop your arms stop at about chest level & "hug a tree", feeling your lungs & ribs expand outward. As you drop your arms slowly to your sides, maintain the lifted rib cage feeling & on into your singing.
- Pretend their is an "invisible string" coming out of the top of your head. Pull on the string & make sure that your head is lifted & free of tension.
- Keep your back straight. The spine should feel lifted & tall.
- Try singing the pitches in the chromatic section again, keeping the spine tall & straight, the head relaxed, & the rib cage lifted. There will be a 100% change in the intonation.

Scoring Commentary

Cause 3: A third appropriate cause is identified and explained.

Remedial Technique for Cause 3: In the description of the solution, the test taker also suggests another aspect of poor posture: tension. The test taker addresses the proper position of the head, arms, rib cage, and spine, supplying both exercises and imagery to achieve this. Once again, the test taker ties the exercises back to the problematic passage to provide closure and to achieve success.

This response demonstrates a full understanding of the musical concepts and processes and earns a score of 5.

Sample Response that Earned a Score of 4

RESPOND TO QUESTION 1 HERE
(Note: You are not required to fill all of the space provided.)

Circle your chosen topic: TOPIC A (specify instrument: ____________) (TOPIC B)

Cause 1:

Poor posture - when singers do not have an aligned posture - they can not breath properly, thus they will flat. Proper posture simply will allow them to take in more air.

Remedial Technique for Cause 1:

Have all of the choir members reach up above their heads and stretch as far as they can. Have them slowly lower their arms and instruct them to keep their rib cage where it is. When their arms are to the side have them relax their shoulders and this will create an open and aligned breathing posture.

Scoring Commentary

Cause 1: The problem of poor posture is identified and how it contributes to flatting is explained.

Remedial Technique for Cause 1: An appropriate exercise is given, but the concept of good posture is implied rather than explained. The test taker says "instruct them to keep their rib cage where it is" but should specify that the rib cage should be raised. Without a clarifying explanation of appropriate posture, students may relax the chest cavity and forfeit the benefits of the exercise if their attention to the specific positioning of the head, spine, and rib cage, is not placed in clearer context.

Cause 2:

Breath control - by releasing breath too quickly or not taking a breath when needed, the pitch can begin to go flat. Either of these can cause an improper air flow.

Remedial Technique for Cause 2:

First start by having the choir do lip buzzes, by buzzing a pitch or short scale for a small amount of time. This will allow them to get a good air flow. In connection with this have them place their hands on their lips or just above them and have them feel their diaphragms expand when breathing in for the lip buzz, telling them to invision filling up an inner tube around their mid section. This whole process will coordinate with proper posture.

Scoring Commentary

Cause 2: The concept of inadequate breath support is explained, although not explicitly identified. The test taker provides enough detail to demonstrate an understanding of a possible problem, even though the precise musical term is not used.

Remedial Technique for Cause 2: Lip buzzing, also called "lip trills" or "motor boat," does not actually allow students to get a "good air flow" as the test taker claims. Lip trills can be executed only if one is already exercising proper breath support. The sequence of the remedial techniques should be reversed to be effective. The students should first understand and experience diaphragmatic breathing before attempting lip trills. The exercise of lip trills would reinforce the proper breathing technique. The application of this skill to the problematic passage should follow. An unambiguous explanation of breath support would also improve this response.

Cause 3:

Sound placement - the shape of their mouth position, or soft palate and resonance chamber may cause their sound to go flat if the soft palate is down or their lips are too spread.

Remedial Technique for Cause 3:

This can very easily be fixed by having the choir hum their line a few times to get their soft palate to raise. Often the hum will bring the sound more forward and cause it to remain in pitch. After this is done have them sing the line, but raise their facial expressions to give them a visual idea of raising the pitch when it goes flat. A proper hum is done with lips barely touching and teeth apart.

Scoring Commentary

Cause 3: The test taker is on the right track but does not identify the problem specifically. Using an appropriate term, rather than blurring several concepts together such as vowel placement, open throat, etc., would improve the response. Fortunately, the test taker's elaboration indicates substantial understanding of the mechanisms at work, such as that the soft palate should be raised and that the mouth position should be addressed.

Remedial Technique for Cause 3: The remedy of humming is debatable, especially as is presented here. Humming would improve the resonance of the tone, but would not necessarily raise the soft palate or correct mouth position. More explanation on how both could be improved is warranted. An exercise focusing on raising the soft palate, such as yawn sighs or the use of imagery suggesting an "open throat," would be more appropriate.

The test taker also mentions "raising facial expressions" to give a "visual idea of raising the pitch." The test taker should clarify what is meant by "raising facial expressions" with examples, such as raising eyebrows. This strategy, however, would help concentration and focus, but not necessarily raise the soft palate or correct mouth position. Additional information to connect this strategy with the cause is needed.

Overall, the test taker demonstrates a substantial understanding of the musical concepts and processes and receives a score of 4.

Sample Response that Earned a Score of 3

RESPOND TO QUESTION 1 HERE
(Note: You are not required to fill all of the space provided.)

Circle your chosen topic: TOPIC A (specify instrument: ___________) (TOPIC B)

Cause 1:

One cause of this flatting could be lack of breath support to sustain the sound.

Remedial Technique for Cause 1:

I would talk to my students about proper breathing and would have them participate in breathing exercises to determine if they are breathing correctly. One such exercise would be to have the students pretend they are wearing inner tubes around their waists. They would inhale with their abdominal muscles (diaphragm expanding to inflate the inner tube). Then I would point to them as if to "pop" the innertube, and the students would then exhale making a constant hissing sound. I would explain that the stomach should go down as the breath goes out, then draw the analogy to the singing voice. We should sustain the sound with the constant steady breath support. This breath support helps us remain in tune as we sing.

Scoring Commentary

Cause 1: This response begins well. The test taker correctly identifies the lack of breath support as a cause.

Remedial Technique for Cause 1: Rather than beginning with a general statement about talking to the students about proper breathing, the test taker should strengthen the response by specifying what to explain to the students, describing what proper breathing is and how to achieve it. By describing the necessity of deep breathing with the diaphragm and maintaining slow, steady exhalation, dependent upon the length of the phrase, the test taker would have demonstrated evidence of a full understanding of the concept. Without such a description, this evidence is lacking. The lack of explanation also weakens the exercise that follows because the instruction on appropriate breathing technique was not developed. Without an understanding of correct breathing, students may do the exercise incorrectly or lack the conceptual framework necessary to apply proper breathing to their singing. The test taker should be careful to specify the processes to ensure students' learning. The test taker should connect the breathing exercise with the intonation problem by practicing the passage while maintaining the same sensation and breathing technique of the exercise. Although the idea is basically on the right track, the process is incomplete because the test taker does not apply the new skills or concepts to the original problem.

Cause 2:

Another cause of flatting could be a lack of vibrato in the voices.

Remedial Technique for Cause 2:

One technique for enhancing vibrato in young voices is to practice humming the song. The humming gives the singer the "buzz" in the mask of the face and helps him feel the proper placement. I would practice the song on a hum, encouraging my students to hum through the musical line.

Scoring Commentary

Cause 2: The test taker incorrectly identifies a lack of vibrato as a cause of flatting. While vibrato, correctly performed, may be linked to proper placement and an energized sound, the test taker does not address these issues in cause 2.

Remedial Technique for Cause 2: The response does address the issues of proper placement in the remedial technique, but the explanation fails to address how the singers should hum correctly. Merely encouraging students to hum, without addressing proper technique, is an ineffective teaching strategy. The students may not achieve proper placement, and by not addressing the correct technique, this strategy may actually encourage more flatting. Providing better context, with instruction about humming or an exercise to create the proper sound and sensation for the students, is needed. Only partial credit can be given for this response.

Cause 3:

Another cause of flatting is under-shooting the pitch as a singer moves up or down the scale. In a capella singing, there is no piano to put the choir back on pitch as they flat the notes slightly.

Remedial Technique for Cause 3:

I would practice whole step and half step scales with my choir. I would practice matching the pitches with the piano and the singing these scales a capella.

I would also practice matching pitches with my choir. I would sing a portion of the song, then have them echo it back to me. This technique helps train the ear to hear the pitch and the progression.

Scoring Commentary

Cause 3: Flatting is the "undershooting of the pitch." This third cause the test taker presents is merely a restatement of the prompt and makes no contribution to the response's score.

Remedial Technique for Cause 3: The practice of singing scales would help address flatting by providing the singers with skill in ear-training. The test taker should also develop this exercise by discussing whether the choir should sing the scales in unison or on different pitches, and by describing how the transition from singing scales to singing the passage would be accomplished. The test taker should use the proper musical terms of whole-tone scale and chromatic scale.

The final exercise also aids listening skills. The test taker could identify this as an echo-singing experience and should indicate specifically how this exercise will "train the ear to hear the pitch and the progression."

Because the test taker presents ideas that were basically correct and demonstrates a basic understanding of the musical concepts and processes, the response earned a score of 3.

Sample Response that Earned a Score of 2

RESPOND TO QUESTION 1 HERE
(Note: You are not required to fill all of the space provided.)

Circle your chosen TOPIC A (specify instrument: ______________) (TOPIC B)

Cause 1:

Pitch (notes). (Correction of notes)

Use piano

Remedial Technique for Cause 1:

In order to correct pitch w/in a piece (a cappella piece). It is best to listen to the students in section first. Starts w/ the sopranos then altos tenors, bass etc. The use of vocalise is important. Whenever they are going flat w/in the song, start there first & make use of the piano so as they can hear their part. When separate the section it makes it easier to hear & find out where the problem area is.

Scoring Commentary

Cause 1: The test taker may not have read the prompt carefully. The prompt indicates that notes have been previously learned. The test taker attempts to address a moot point, and receives no credit.

Remedial Technique for Cause 1: The technique offered provides a solution to the problem described by the prompt. The isolation of vocal parts can aid the ability of the section to hear their part clearly and correct wrong pitches, but the prompt didn't ask about that. The test taker also mentions the use of vocalises but gives no example of what kind to use and no description of how they would be used to solve the problem.

Cause 2:

Tonality (listening)

Remedial Technique for Cause 2:

Soprano tenor tend to go sharp whereas altos base tend to go flat. Make use of the piano within the altos and bass players their parts separately. Tell them to listen and focus on their indevijual notes within the song. Through vocalize show students the placement of the tone through use of a chart or through use of examples (singing the pitch or again play the pitches and have students sing along without the accompanist).

Scoring Commentary

Cause 2: The response is too brief and provides no support or context to indicate that the concept is understood. The test taker could have meant to identify poor listening skills as a cause but the information is too vague. Clues to the intention are revealed in the solution, but failure to identify or specify a cause will cost credit. The test taker may have had the right idea, but fails to use the proper musical terms. Without additional context, this response provides little evidence that the concept is understood. The response does, however, appear to provide an inaccurate and misleading definition of tonality.

Remedial Technique for Cause 2: The test taker reveals a limited understanding of vocal techniques by making unwarranted generalizations regarding the voice types. The inability to relate the generalization to the concept weakens the response. The test taker revisits the strategy, already used in addressing cause 1, of isolating vocal parts. Because the question requires three different remedial techniques, no credit can be given for the same remedial technique cited twice. In this explanation, as in cause 1, the test taker does mention a vocalise to demonstrate placement but provides no supporting context. The mere mention of a chart and examples without a description provides little genuine evidence that the test taker understands the concept or has a definite solution in mind. The last statement of playing pitches and having the student sing along with accompaniment seems to reiterate the strategy presented earlier.

Cause 3:

Harmony

Remedial Technique for Cause 3:

Play all play using playing. 1st separately than all together. Having choir listen then give the starting pitches for each section and play along with choir 1st then with piano. 1st give pitches. Telling students to listen to there section.

Scoring Commentary

Cause 3: This cause is too vague to receive credit.

Remedial Technique for Cause 3: This remedial technique is another variation of the same strategy discussed in remedial technique 1. The test taker should develop different rehearsal techniques to demonstrate knowledge of various ways to handle a common performance problem.

The test taker, having demonstrated only a limited understanding of the concepts and processes in a choral rehearsal, receives a score of 2.

Sample Response that Earned a Score of 1

RESPOND TO QUESTION 1 HERE
(Note: You are not required to fill all of the space provided.)

Circle your chosen topic: TOPIC A (specify instrument: __________) (TOPIC B)

Cause 1:

The first obvious reason is that this is a "beginning" high school choir. These voices may not be mature enough to sing chromatics in an a cappella piece of music, especially if the music has a high tessitura.

Remedial Technique for Cause 1:

If the music allows, I would begin the piece in a lower key so the voices would not have "strain". I would work very intensely with these beginning voices and play the piano with them every time they sang the song until they could stay in the key that I begin them. A cappella is very difficult even for an advanced high school or even some college choirs.

Scoring Commentary

Cause 1: An appropriate cause for the musical problem has not been identified. By addressing the vocal immaturity of the choir, the response is merely restating the prompt. This response indicates little or no understanding of vocal technique or choral rehearsal techniques.

Remedial Technique for Cause 1: Lowering the pitch may be an initial step in addressing the problem, but as described here it is not an adequate solution. The test taker fails to indicate how lowering the pitch will help to prevent the flatting and makes no mention of returning to the correct pitch.

The test taker suggests using piano accompaniment, but this technique sidesteps the problem of poor intonation with a cappella singing. This may be used as an initial step, but the solution must be developed. The transition from singing with piano accompaniment to singing a cappella without flatting must be addressed. The last statement is irrelevant and should be omitted.

Cause 2:

Another possible reason would be that possibly the choir is singing too much before you rehearse this piece of music. If you wait until the end of the rehearsal the students voices may be "tired".

Remedial Technique for Cause 2:

Move this piece of music to the beginning of rehearsal and don't dwell on the high tessitura part. Yes, you will have to work on this section, but don't "pound" it into the students head. Work on it for a while and then put it away. Maybe have section rehearsals to vary the rehearsal time. Make it more of a pleasant thing rather than an "oh no here comes that awful part that we all hate and don't sing very well."

Scoring Commentary

Cause 2: The second cause is given as vocal fatigue. This is an example where the test taker assumes information not contained in the prompt. The prompt will always provide the essential information. The test taker should identify substantial causes of the problem, such as a lack of energy or poor concentration skills.

Remedial Technique for Cause 2: The response fails to demonstrate knowledge of vocal technique and rehearsal technique and resorts again to merely sidestepping the problem. Psychological factors may, on a generic level, contribute to any musical problem, but the question asks for specific causes and solutions to the problem of flatting. None are provided.

Cause 3:

Another possible reason may be the weather! If you're having a long bout with dark or gloomy weather it can cause a choir not to perform at its best and flatten most music especially that with lots of chromatics and a high tessitura.

Remedial Technique for Cause 3:

Of course you can't wait until its bright and sunny outside to perform every piece of music. But if you start to hear the choir not be able to stay in a key you may want to think about putting off this piece of music until a later date. Then when you get some better weather bring out and work on it then, or if you don't have that weather then try to either lift the "mud" of the rehearsal or possibly think about changing to an easier piece of music.

Scoring Commentary

Cause 3: To demonstrate knowledge about vocal production and ensemble singing, the test taker should address what the students are doing, or not doing, that is causing the pitch to flat. The last cause the test taker supplies, bad weather, is a poor choice because, once again, this factor is not indicated in the prompt. Consequently, the test taker fails to discuss a performance problem genuinely related to flatting. By addressing superficial issues, the test taker demonstrates little or no knowledge of the musical concepts and processes at work in a choral rehearsal.

Remedial Technique for Cause 3: To address flatting in the performance of this a cappella piece, the response proposes two solutions: either wait for better weather or eschew this particular piece altogether in favor of an easier one. The response reveals neither knowledge of choral rehearsal technique nor understanding of appropriate ways to improve students' singing.

By not adhering to the information provided in the prompt, the test taker emphasizes nonmusical causes and demonstrates little or no understanding of the musical concepts and processes involved in the problem. Although the topics raised by the response are tangentially related to ensemble intonation, the solutions are undeveloped, superficial, irrelevant, or professionally irresponsible. This response receives a score of 1.

Chapter 12

Sample Responses to Question 2 of *Music: Concepts and Processes* and How They Were Scored

► ► ► ► ► ► ► ► ► ► ► ►

Music: Concepts and Processes

Question 2—General Music

This question tests your ability to sequence learning and demonstrate your knowledge of general music concepts, appropriate musical selections from different cultural origins and musical traditions, and teaching strategies.

Study the following sample responses and commentary by the scorers.

Sample Response that Earned a Score of 5

RESPOND TO QUESTION 2 HERE
(Note: You are not required to fill all of the space provided.)

Task I: Grade or grade range: 7th grade

Task II: Briefly describe an appropriate and logical instructional sequence (include TWO musical selections from different cultural origins or musical traditions and ONE or more participatory experiences).

1. Have students listen as you play a major scale on the piano. Then have them listen as you play a minor scale.
2. Ask the students if the two scales were the same or different. See if they can describe how they were different. Expect answers such as major = happy, minor = sad.
3. Provide a handout with a major and minor scale reproduced on a staff. ex. C Major or C Minor.
4. Have students in pairs locate all of the whole steps and half steps in each scale. Have pairs share answers with class.
5. Explain to students which scales are major and minor based on the half step and whole step pattern.
6. Once they have identified the pattern of a both scales have them create a major scale using a staff on the board.
7. Ask volunteers to see if they can alter the scale to make it minor.
Play through each of the scales throughout the lesson to familiarize the students with the tonalities

8. Play a variety of musical selections that are in both major and minor keys. Give students a call chart and have them listen and decide whether each piece is major or minor. Some selctions to include may be:

Major	Minor
The Ashgrove	Scarborough Fair
The Star Spangled Banner	The Canoe Song
Frere Jacque	When Johnny Comes Marching Home

9. Listen to each song again giving the correct answers, or asking students to share their results.
10. Collect call charts and use for assessment.

Task III: Briefly describe an additional activity that reinforces what you taught about major and minor modes in Task II.

1. Print out the names of specific keys on slips of paper. ex. A major A minor, C major, C minor, etc.
2. Have each student draw a slip of paper and create a scale based on what key they pick.
3. Give students the opportunity to use the piano and other instruments to create a melody using only the notes on their particular scale. The melody should be a specified length 8 to 16 measures.
3. Have students hand in composition at the end of class.
4. After teacher has looked over compositions and located any errors she will return the melodies to the students.
5. Students will then have the opportunity to make any necessary changes.
6. Let students perform melodies for the class.
7. When not performing the students should decide whether the melody being played is major or minor.

Scoring Commentary

This response begins with an appropriate preparatory activity wherein students are asked to listen to and compare the differences between a major and minor scale played on the piano. The instructional sequence proceeds logically and smoothly, as students identify the whole- and half-step pattern of a major and minor scale, create major and minor scales, and then identify pieces as major or minor. The test taker should have identified the order of the whole and half steps for each scale for clarity, but overall the test taker demonstrates a full understanding of the processes involved in teaching the concept. The test taker also demonstrates familiarity with various musical traditions by citing examples of folksongs of English, French, and Native American cultures, and American patriotic songs. The additional activity reinforces the concept of major and minor tonality as students first create assigned scales, then compose melodies based on those scales. Although 8 to 16 measures may be rather long for such an assignment, the assignment itself is an excellent activity to acquaint the students with the tones that constitute the major and minor scales. Sharing their compositions allows the students another opportunity to hear and identify major and minor melodies.

This response demonstrates a full understanding of the concepts and processes, and it receives a score of 5.

Sample Response that Earned a Score of 4

RESPOND TO QUESTION 2 HERE
(Note: You are not required to fill all of the space provided.)

Task I: Grade or grade range: secondary 9-12 (grades)

Task II: Briefly describe an appropriate and logical instructional sequence (include TWO musical selections from different cultural origins or musical traditions and ONE or more participatory experiences).

1. A major mode, do re me fa sol la ti do, should be practiced with the curwen hand signals while singing.
2. Notationally, the concepts of modes should be taugh, having each student know each mode (Ionian, Dorian, Phyrigian, Lydian, Mixolydian, Aeolian, and Locrian). Using the key of C for example, the students should be able to write the major scale and the pattern of half and whole steps between each scale degree. They should be able to do this for every mode. i.e.,

Dorian = w w h w w w h

Aeolian = w h w w h w w

3. To introduce the minor mode, simply state that the minor mode is the 6th mode, Aeolian. In relation to whole and half steps, explain that the Aeolian (natural minor) has a half-step lowered 3rd, 6th, and 7th scale degree.
4. The 1st musical selection to sing with solfege then in French is "Frere Jacques".

Text:	Fre-re	Ja-cques,	Fre-re	Ja-cques	dor-mez	vou
scale degrees:	1 2	3 1	1 2	3 1	3 4	5
Curwen hand signals/solfege:	do re	mi do	do re	mi do	mi fa	sol

*This is example if the major (Ionian Mode)

5. The 2nd musical example to share with the class would be a recording of the Bach C minor prelude. Give them a copy of the piece and walk through the chords, explaining the chordal structure and compiling a work sheet designed to have the students create minor and major chord as home-work.

Task III: Briefly describe an additional activity that reinforces what you taught about major and minor modes in Task II.

Using the piano, play random major and minor chords. Have the students raise their hands to answer, and don't stop until every student has answered a chord correctly. You can advance this by play random musical examples of songs, concertos, sonatas, etc..., and have the students respond in the same manner.

Scoring Commentary

The lesson begins promisingly with students singing a major scale, complemented with hand signals and solfège sylables to underpin the concept of scale degrees. The pattern of whole and half steps is presented for the major and minor modes with notation examples. This demonstrates evidence of the test taker's understanding of the musical concept. Because the test taker explains the minor mode in detail, mentioning the lowered third, sixth, and seventh scale degrees, and uses the appropriate musical terms of Aeolian mode and natural minor, the test taker provides further evidence of a substantial knowledge of the musical concepts. The error describing the interval pattern of the major scale as "Dorian" appears to be a slip of the pen, since it is corrected in step 4, where it is correctly described as "Ionian."

The test taker introduces all the modes through notation. A more musical (and current) approach would be to sing each mode or present a piece or an excerpt in the mode, identify the notes involved, and then identify the half-and whole-step relationships. Introducing all modes at this level, especially mixed with misleading Medieval nomenclature (Glarean has Aeolian as mode 9, not 6), would be overwhelming for the students. The test taker could have limited the lesson to the introduction of only the major and minor modes.

The test taker chooses an elementary-level folk song as an example of major tonality, rather than a musical selection appropriate for this grade level. The musical selection serving as the example of the minor tonality, on the other hand, is better suited for the high school students.

The participatory experiences are weak. The test taker suggests involving the students in singing a major scale, writing the pattern of half and whole steps for each mode, and singing "Frere Jacques." At a high school level, students should be expected to participate on a more sophisticated level. The activity mentioned in step five, guided exploration of the chordal structure of the Bach piece, would be more appropriate for high school students. The test taker, however, does not provide enough explanation to transition the students from identifying scales to identifying and creating chords. In addition, this activity is not necessarily participatory, seeming to be a worksheet assignment.

The additional activity that reinforces major and minor chords is also weak. The identification of random major and minor chords would be better accomplished by having the students respond on a worksheet. Among other reasons, if students must wait for everyone to have a chance to answer, they will lose interest and focus. The test taker could improve the response by suggesting a list of specific works for the major and minor examples that could be played.

While the test taker demonstrates a substantial knowledge of the musical concepts, the sequence of instruction contains some weaknesses and the processes are not fully developed. This response receives a score of 4.

Sample Response that Earned a Score of 3

RESPOND TO QUESTION 2 HERE
(Note: You are not required to fill all of the space provided.)

Task I: Grade or grade range: 9–12

Task II: Briefly describe an appropriate and logical instructional sequence (include TWO musical selections from different cultural origins or musical traditions and ONE or more participatory experiences).

After explaining what we were about to learn I would sing two short well known melodies one minor and major. Students would listen for minor/major "feeling." Next we would sing as a group a minor and a major scale while looking at the same. Students would be shown how the scales differ in their notation and how this effects the sound. Next we would sing The Third Comes in two sizes from Sing Legato by Jennings. After students can sing and recognize a minor scale, major scale, a minor third and a major third, we would proceed to guided listening. Students would listen to Handel's "Halleluyah Chorus" and the Ukrainian carol Nebo c Zeiul to note the strong major and minor modes. Next we would listen to Boiutines I feel like a motherless child and Everytime I feel the spirit, then sing them to reinforce the different major and minor sounds. For homework, students would be asked to identify 2 popular tunes one major and one minor and if possible bring in recordings. Each students examples should be played and the class as a whole should identify the mode. Next, students should listen to a symphonic work with major and minor passages and be asked to identify when the piece modulates. Perhaps candy could be given as prizes or the class could work in teams like as on a game show. At this point a thorough review of what has been learned should occur. Students should be "quizzed" to check for understanding. If possible scores should be provided and students should be asked to identify whether the composition is major or minor without hearing it. If they cannot, then the "spelling" of major and minor chords must be taught once student's are making "good" guesses play the scores so they can hear and see the effect of the third on the tonality. A closing listening can be Straus' Thus Spoke Zartosta (theme from 2001) with it's bold major and minor chords. Encourage students to exalt in the major and morn in the minor. i.e., have fun!

Task III: Briefly describe an additional activity that reinforces what you taught about major and minor modes. in Task II.

As a more advanced activity students should be divided into 3 groups based on their voicing (as closely as possible in a general music class): Group 1 = the men, 2 = lower female voices; 3 = higher females. Students should practice building major and minor chords in Root position as well as a first and second inversions. This vocal challenge can be great fun once students get over stage fright. Each group must have a chance to "find" the third, both major and minor. Most likely students will find root position. The fun starts with inversions. This activity reinforces the difference between the modes by having the students build the modes themselves. The students must determine the right third and "time" the mode. Additionally, students could modulate by raising or lowering the third to instantly hear the difference. Not all singers will have good ears or voices, so keep the lesson upbeat and jovial. Perhaps each group could choose a champion and these three could build triads and the class could identify their mode as quickly as possible. It would be easy to bridge to dimished and argumented triads from this lesson.

Scoring Commentary

The instructional sequence the test taker suggests appears, basically, to be appropriate and logical, but details are lacking. The test taker begins by singing a minor and a major melody but doesn't specify the songs. The test taker loses some credibility by remaining too general. Asking the students to listen for a "minor/major feeling" is a vague activity that does not provide evidence that the test taker understands the concept or the process of explaining major and minor tonality to students.

By suggesting that the students sing and read the notation of a major and a minor scale, the test taker begins to focus the students' learning, but then the test taker quickly returns to a vague reference, "students would be shown how the scales differ in their notation and how this affects the sound." Instead, the test taker should discuss what steps the teacher should take in order for this learning to take place.

The test taker mentions that the student will be able to sing a major and minor scale, plus a major and minor third, but does not stipulate how each of these skills is to be mastered.

The guided listening experience seems to be without structure. To simply listen to pieces without some kind of expected response—written, verbal, or group—would not hold students' attention or interest, and the test taker fails to provide a structure for this activity.

Just singing songs in major and minor tonalities does not reinforce the difference between the tonalities. The specific instruction sequence, including steps leading to a discussion of the differences, should be presented.

Playing everyone's recording would be impractical and would take too long, unless only an excerpt of each was played. How the "class as a whole" will identify the mode should be explained. Without clarifying context, this does not seem to be an appropriate learning experience.

Asking the students to identify when the piece modulates demonstrates some lack of understanding of the musical concepts and teaching processes. Modulation is a complex, sophisticated concept. Much more than major and minor modes would need to be taught before students could hope to identify modulations. The test taker's idea of working in teams like a game show needs to be further developed. No credit can be given to an idea that is presented without any details to explain its purpose and how it would be executed.

Asking the students to identify whether the composition is major or minor by looking at scores is another example of a lack of understanding of process. Students cannot be expected to identify major and minor tonality in notation unless they have been taught how to do so. The test taker fails to realize the necessary processes involved in understanding this concept.

The additional activity is too advanced without additional preparation. The test taker should explain how this activity would be presented to the students.

Because the test taker has been too general in the descriptions of the learning activities and has not presented the activities in a logical sequence of instruction, only a basic understanding of the concepts and the processes is evident. This response receives a score of 3.

Sample Response that Earned a Score of 2

RESPOND TO QUESTION 2 HERE
(Note: You are not required to fill all of the space provided.)

Task I: Grade or grade range: 1st

Task II: Briefly describe an appropriate and logical instructional sequence (include TWO musical selections from different cultural origins or musical traditions and ONE or more participatory experiences).

To begin I would ask the class if they knew what the word "mood" meant. After their responses I would go on to say that people can be in good, happy moods, angry moods, sad moods etc. I would ask them what mood they were in. Then I would explain that music had moods too. Music can be happy or sad and listening to music can make you feel happy or sad. I would tell them words we use for happy & music major.

I would then play "Humoreske" on a recording. I would ask them if the music sounded happy/major or sad/minor. We would discuss why they thought the music sounded happy (bouncey, lively, etc.). I would then play "Moonlight Sonata" on a recording. I would again ask them if they thought it was happy or sad. We would on a recording. I would again ask them if they thought it was happy or sad. We would discuss why they thought it was sad. I would then go over to the piano. I would ask them listen to some more examples. I would ask them to smile if they thought the music was (happy) major or pretend to cry if we thought the music was (sad) minor. I would then play 5–8 short examples such as "If you're happy and you know it", "Jimmy Crack Corn" and "Swanee". To wake up the class I would ask them to come up with some songs they were happy and sad. We would then sing some of them. I would end by asking if they remembered what words we used to describe happy and sad music.

Hopefully some of them would remember the words "major and minor". This would take plass in a single 30 minute class period.

CONTINUE TO RESPOND TO QUESTION 2 HERE
(Note: You are not required to fill all of the space provided.)

Task III: Briefly describe an additional activity that reinforces what you taught about major and minor modes in Task II.

In the next music class I would review the words "major" and "minor". I would ask who remembered what they meant. After their response I would pass out the worksheets. They would have two boxes on them. I would explain to the kids that they would draw a picture of something happy while they listened to "morning" (Grieg) and then after a while they would draw a picture of something sad while they listened to "Ase's Death"

I would mention the titles of the pieces but put most emphasis on whether they were major or minor. This would take about twenty minutes including crayons & paper pass-out and pick-up. I would complete the class by having them think of ways to move that showed they were sad and ways to move that showed they were happy. I would play "Nobody likes me" for minor music and "Tippy Toes" (music K-8 magazine) to end with a song in "major."

Scoring Commentary

This response begins addressing major and minor modes through a comparison of "happy" and "sad" moods. While this is an understandable means of beginning an instructional sequence for students of this age, the test taker should develop the musical meaning and context to include a fundamental concept of major and minor modes. However, no development of the concept ensues. By emphasizing the mood of the music instead of the sound, this teaching sequence may promote students' misconception of the terms *major* and *minor:* students could misconstrue the terms to refer to a description of how music makes them feel, rather than how the music actually sounds. Instruction should be given addressing the difference between the sound of a major chord or scale and a minor chord or scale. Because the instructional sequence does not lead to a musical understanding of the concepts of major and minor modes, little evidence is given that the musical concept of major and minor modes is understood. The test taker's knowledge appears to be limited.

The test taker suggests playing "Humoresque" and "Moonlight Sonata," both of which are classical pieces that would be too long and complex to serve as primary examples for a first grade class. Choosing musical selections more appropriate for the selected grade level would have strengthened the response.

The participatory activity of smiling or "pretending to cry" to identify happy or sad music reinforces the mood of the music rather than the appropriate tonality. Students could be easily distracted with the charades, mimic what others are doing, and benefit little from the listening experience. The folksongs the test taker suggests as examples are all in major tonalities; some examples should have been in minor.

The test taker asks students to "come up with some songs they know" to identify as happy and sad. Generally, students in first grade would have a limited background in minor modes and may experience difficulty in recalling minor-key songs.

The additional activity of drawing something happy or sad while listening to long selections of music would be inappropriate to reinforce the concept of major and minor modes. While a multi-subject approach is laudable, the test taker has not yet provided students with a deeper musical understanding of major and minor modes. A more appropriate activity would be for the children to hear excerpts and circle the correct mode. To strengthen such a response, the test taker could provide a list of possible excerpts, including music from different cultures or historical periods.

This response demonstrates a limited knowledge about the musical concepts and processes, and it receives a score of 2.

Sample Response that Earned a Score of 1

RESPOND TO QUESTION 2 HERE
(Note: You are not required to fill all of the space provided.)

Task I: Grade or grade range: 9th

Task II: Briefly describe an appropriate and logical instructional sequence (include TWO musical selections from different cultural origins or musical traditions and ONE or more participatory experiences).

This lesson would be taught over one period of instruction. I would begin the class period with recording of the "Bridal March" from Lohengrin. I would ask the students if they have heard the piece; show it makes them feel a where they have heard. Many of them should know it from weddings but for those who don't I will inform. Weddings are very happy occasions and the music is used to reflect that happy occassion. I would explain to the students that music that evokes a happy feeling or its makes you feel good is described as having a major tonality.

After that I would play the "Darth Vader" theme from Star Wars and ask them the same questions I asked about the "Bridal March." I would then show a clip of the movie where this music was used. I would then ask the students to describe that particular scene, which is of Darth Vader explaining his evil plan. I would then explain to the students that music used to describe sad bad or unhappy events is classified as having minor tonality. To encourage class participation I would put the students into cooperative learning groups for a tonality identification game. I would go to the piano and randomly play major and minor tonality chords and the would have to respond by raising the correct sign with right answer. The winning team would receive extra credit.

Another experience I would use is to have the students bring in a copy of Romeo and Juliet which they read in the ninth grade. I would divide them into groups and give them specific scenes to pick tonalities that would best reflect the emotion of that scene to someone that has never read the story before.

Task III: Briefly describe an additional activity that reinforces what you taught about major and minor modes in Task II.

One additional activity that I would use is to have the students watch their favorite movie and try to classify the music heard in the background as major or minor according to the action taking place.

Scoring Commentary

No musical concepts are presented in the lesson, and the materials presented in this response are not appropriate for the grade level the test taker has selected. At this level, students should be expected to understand differences between major and minor modes through instruction in music theory. Rather than addressing contrasting moods, the test taker could focus on the contrasting sounds of the major and minor modes and explain the differences between the scale patterns or the tonic chords of each in a logical sequence.

The musical examples do little to illuminate either mood or the musical concept. The Darth Vader theme in particular is likely to generate confusion: It begins with a descending major third and the opening motive outlines a major triad.

The test taker describes two participatory experiences, both of which are inappropriate for the age level and for the development of the musical concept. Requiring students to identify major and minor chords by raising a sign in a cooperative learning situation may be appropriate for early elementary grades, but not for ninth grade. Identifying dramatic scenes as having a major or minor tonality emphasizes a non-musical understanding of the concepts of major and minor, relegating these harmonies to be synonyms for "happy" and "sad" situations. Expecting the students to identify the different modes, without the instruction or background required to tell the two modes apart, is unrealistic and would only contribute to the students' frustration.

The additional activity is also a poor choice because the emphasis is on developing an understanding of major and minor through dramatic situations, rather than through aural training or theoretical understanding. The activity is poorly explained and would be confusing and frustrating to the students if it were assigned as written here; students could not be expected to comment on the background music of an entire movie, or be able to simply classify the entire background music as major or minor. The test taker needs to be more specific and think through the processes involved.

This response indicates little or no understanding of the musical concepts and processes, and it received a score of 1.

Chapter 13

Preparing for the *Music: Analysis* Test

► ► ► ► ► ► ► ► ► ► ► ►

The goal of this chapter is to provide you with strategies for preparing to read, analyze, and understand the questions on the *Music: Analysis* test and to write successful responses. In a later chapter, you will see actual responses by test takers to a question from the test and an expert scorer's explanation of why each response received the score it did.

Introduction to the Question Types

The *Analysis* test consists of three questions. As with the *Concepts and Processes* examination, you shouldn't worry about writing an essay. Your responses are *not* scored on writing style, only on the correctness of the content.

The first two questions ask you to listen to recordings of an instrumental ensemble and a choral ensemble, each performing a short piece. After you listen to each performance and follow the musical score, you must identify five errors. Each performance is played five times, and there are typically nine to twelve errors built into each performance, so you'll have plenty of time and opportunity to find five errors. The errors you are to identify include the following:

- imbalance among instruments or voices
- incorrect accents
- incorrect articulation
- incorrect interpretation of dynamic or tempo markings

DO NOT describe errors in *pitch*, *rhythm*, or *diction*. The directions are clear about this, yet test takers occasionally still do write about them. Don't lose points by writing about these kinds of errors.

The errors to look for are, frankly, blatant departures from the scores as written, so don't focus on fine, subjective points of interpretation such as the following:

Measure(s)	Description
21	not enough rallentando - should be rounder

Sometimes test takers respond with the kind of subjective interpretation shown above and lose points. This is not a test of your personal interpretive tastes. Rather, it tests your ability to recognize performance errors, so stick with describing genuine errors—departures from the score as written. Keep in mind that one musician's "not enough" is another's "too much." If a rallentando is marked in the music and the ensemble performs a rallentando, then they have *not* departed from the score as written. If in the same measure the bassoon is belting out notes fortissimo when the part is marked pianissimo, point that out instead. If the ensemble *completely misses* a rallentando, or if they speed up instead, that's a legitimate error and you should point it out.

You need to identify the location of the errors in the score by the measure number (the numbers are printed in the scores for your convenience) and to provide a brief description of each. The response space is set up as an easy-to-use form for you to fill in—you can see it in the sample response booklet in appendix F.

While your description can and should be brief, be sure to specify the kind of error and the part in which it occurs. Also be sure to use appropriate musical terminology. In the performance for Question 2, for example, if you hear a tenor singing unmarked accents on the weak beats in measures 5 and 6, don't write something like this:

Measure(s)	Description
4–7	men wrong beats

That response is inaccurate and vague and loses points. Instead, write something more like this:

Measure(s)	Description
5–6	tenors accent weak beats

The third question offers a choice of three topics:

- instrumental music
- choral music
- general music

Choose only ONE topic—the one with which you are most comfortable and familiar—and concentrate on writing a good response to all of the tasks the question poses. Some test takers unnecessarily give answers for more than one topic. A few do well on two or all three, but this does not earn them more points. Concentrate on just one topic and do the best you can on it.

For the instrumental and choral questions, you are asked to examine two scores and to determine the following for each:

- the appropriate school level (elementary, middle/junior high, senior high)
- the appropriate ensemble
- instrumental ensembles, such as concert band, jazz band, or orchestra
- vocal ensembles, such as mixed chorus, girls' choir, boys' choir, show choir, madrigal/chamber choir, treble choir
- the stylistic influences, for which you should identify significant characteristics indicating the historical period, genre, or the cultural origin
- two performance challenges unique to each piece you would anticipate
- appropriate rehearsal techniques to help students meet each challenge

These last two—the performance challenges and how you would address them—are where you can earn most of your points. Be sure to identify genuine performance challenges unique to each piece. You should identify the measure(s), the part, and the specific problem you anticipate. Be clear about how you would approach the problem.

Avoid writing about generic problems or simply rewording the performance challenge. Also avoid making things up. The test scorers are experienced music educators, and they score the question in their specialty: band and orchestra directors score 3A, choral directors 3B, general/elementary music educators score 3C. They can tell when a response is not straightforward.

Similarly, for the general music question (3C), you are asked to examine two pieces and to determine the following for each:

- the appropriate grade level
- a rationale for the grade level chosen
- the stylistic influences (name significant characteristics that identify the historical period, the genre, or the cultural origin)
- three musical concepts that would be most appropriately demonstrated using the example for the grade level you selected
- a specific explanation of how the example could be successfully used to teach each concept

Although the directions specify, and the response space reemphasizes, that both examples are to be analyzed, test takers occasionally are confused and don't know what to do. Be perfectly clear on this matter: you need to analyze *both* examples for your topic in your response.

What to Study

Your success on this test is determined by your ability to do the following:

- listen alertly and critically to musical performances
- analyze musical scores for stylistic influences
- exercise knowledge and understanding of appropriate repertoire levels
- anticipate performance challenges and formulate rehearsal techniques for meeting these challenges (for choices A and B)
- identify musical concepts and specific teaching opportunities (for choice C)

Consider the following areas for review:

Principles of score analysis

Score reading, including interpretation of notation and symbols, and stylistic interpretation:

- Know how to read and "hear what you see" on the pages of instrumental and choral scores.
- Be familiar with tempo, articulation, and dynamic markings.
- Be able to identify instrumental and vocal ensembles.
- Be familiar with characteristics that identify the score's historical period or cultural origin and its genre.

Principles of score interpretation (Question 3—Topics A or B)

Be familiar with the following:

- common phrasing and balance practices in instrumental and choral ensembles
- choral performance practices, vocal development and technique, including voicing of standard ensembles, principles of good vocal production and choral training
- instrumental performance practices, development, and techniques, including instrumentation of standard ensembles, principles of good sound production and ensemble playing
- common performance challenges in a variety of musical genres
- appropriate rehearsal techniques to meet specific performance challenges

Principles of teaching general music (Question 3—Topic C)

- Be familiar with the music elements that provide a framework for learning music concepts such as melody, harmony, rhythm, timbre, texture, and form.
- Be able to identify musical concepts demonstrated in a variety of styles representative of the repertoire of general music classes.
- Be familiar with appropriate teaching strategies for teaching musical concepts found in a musical score.

The Analysis General Scoring Guide

Questions 1 and 2, Critical Listening, will be scored according to the following scoring guide:

The score range is 0 to 5.

Each error (including location and description) equals 1 point.

- If the description is an adequate explanation of an error that occurs in the measures(s) indicated, 1 point is awarded.
- If the description is not adequate or is a description of an element that is not in error, no point is awarded.

Question 3, Score Analysis, will be scored according to the following scoring guide:

The score range is 0 to 10.

Points are distributed as follows:

- Instrumental Music or Choral Music (Topics A or B, respectively)

  For each excerpt:

  - ❒ 1 point: for the discussion of stylistic influences in the piece
  - ❒ 2 points: 1 point for each correctly identified, accurately described, significant performance challenge. The challenge must be appropriate for the school level selected by the test taker.
  - ❒ 2 points: 1 point for each rehearsal technique described to help students meet each challenge. The challenge must be appropriate for the school level selected by the test taker.

  Points for both excerpts will be added together for the total score.

- General Music (Topic C)

  For each piece:

  - ❒ 1 point: for circling a suitable grade level for each piece and defending the selection
  - ❒ 1 point: discussing stylistic influences in the piece
  - ❒ 3 points: 1 point for identifying each musical concept and explaining how the piece would be used to teach that concept. The concept and demonstration must be appropriate for the school level circled.

  Points you earned for both pieces will be added together for your total score.

Chapter 14

Practice Test, *Music: Analysis*

► ► ► ► ► ► ► ► ► ► ► ►

Now that you have studied the strategies for answering *Music: Analysis* questions, you can try the following practice test. You might find it helpful to simulate actual testing conditions, giving yourself 60 minutes to work on the questions.

Where To Write Your Answers

Appendix F provides you with the response space in which to write your answers. These pages are formatted just like the response space you will get inside your test book when you take the actual test. For the actual test, the printed music is in a booklet called the Question Insert that you can remove so you can look at the music for each question as you write. For this practice test, you can simulate the conditions of the actual test by cutting out the pages of appendix F and photocopying them. Then use the rest of this chapter as the Question Insert, and use your copy of appendix F as the response space of your test book. This not only will allow you to look at the music in the present chapter as you write your answers, it also will let you write on a clean copy of the response space each time you try the practice test.

We want to provide you with a practice test that is as similar as possible to the actual test you will take. To that end, the directions on the CD are exactly like those of one of the actual tests, including the page numbers mentioned in the directions. The practice test in this chapter reflects those page numbers. The page numbers you will hear in the directions are shown in bold (e.g., page 5) at the bottom of the page. These appear above the dark bar that shows the running page numbers of the whole study guide. Although the test you actually take may differ slightly in this regard, it will be very similar to the practice test.

The Practice Test

For Questions 1 and 2 (Critical Listening), follow along with the CD starting with track 28 (please see appendix C). Remember that for Question 3 (Score Analysis) you need to choose only ONE of the topics (A, B, or C).

When you have finished the practice test, you can compare your responses to the sample responses in chapter 15. In that chapter, each sample response is followed by analytical remarks provided by one of the test's chief scorers.

Keep in mind that the questions on the test you take at an actual administration will be based on different music, although the tasks in each question will be approximately the same.

THE PRAXIS SERIES

Professional Assessments for Beginning Teachers®

TEST NAME:

Music: Analysis Practice Questions

Time—60 Minutes

3 Questions

Questions 1 and 2

Approximate time—30 minutes

Directions:

Two musical scores are printed in this Question Insert beginning on page 5. For each score, you will hear a performance that contains errors, that is, departures from the score as written.

The errors you are to identify include:

- imbalance among instruments or voices
- incorrect accents
- incorrect articulation
- incorrect interpretation of dynamic or tempo markings

Do not identify errors in pitch, rhythm, or diction.

Using the forms provided on pages 4 and 5 of your Test Book, identify and describe five different errors in each performance. Write the measure number(s) where each error occurs and write a brief description of each error. Below is a sample of how you would write the location and description of the errors in your Test Book.

Sample Response

Location of Error by Measure Number(s)	Description of Error
1. 3–4	winds missed slurs
2. 7–10	no dynamic change
3. 31–35	accompaniment out of balance
4. 15	inappropriate accents (brass)
5. 27–28	tempo drags

You may make notes on the scores, but only the answers you write on pages 4 and 5 of the Test Book will be judged.

Each performance will be played five times, with a brief pause after each of the first four playings. A longer pause will follow the final playing of each performance to allow you time to complete your answers in the Test Book. You will also be given a moment to look through the score before the first playing.

We will now begin the test. Turn to the musical score for Question 1, which begins on page 5 of this Question Insert, and to the answer form on page 4 of the Test Book.

-4-

Musical score for QUESTION 1.

-5-

QUESTION 1 — Continued

-6-

Musical score for QUESTION 2.

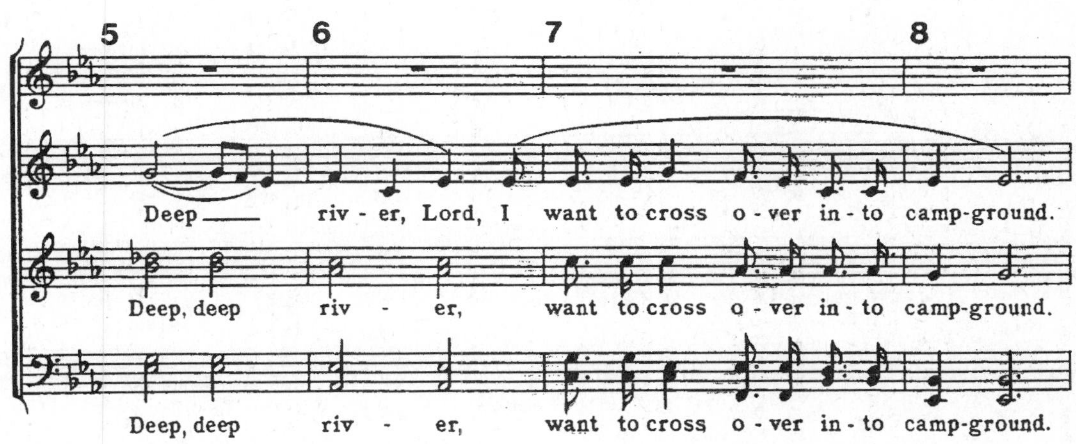

-7-

QUESTION 2 — Continued

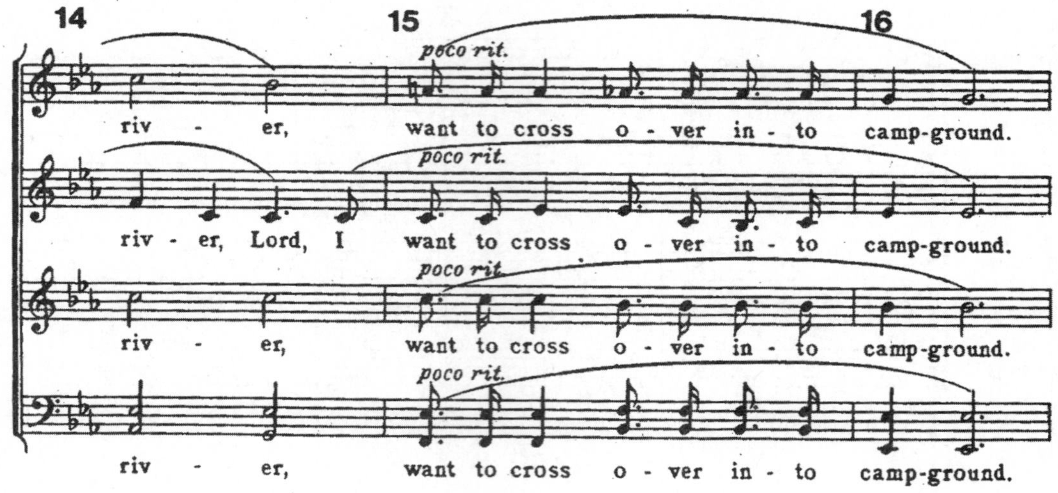

-8-

Question 3

30 minutes

Directions:

Choose and respond to one of the three topics presented below. Be sure to begin your response on the page designated for the topic you choose.

TOPIC A: INSTRUMENTAL MUSIC

Examine both instrumental examples on pages 11–12 of this Question Insert.

For each example:

- Circle the appropriate school level and ensemble type on the lists in your Test Book.
- Identify and briefly describe the stylistic influences in the example, such as folk, ethnic, cultural, and/or historical characteristics.
- Identify and describe two significant performance challenges in the example. (Specify measure number(s).)
- Describe in detail appropriate rehearsal techniques to assist students in meeting each challenge.

Begin your response on page 6 of your Test Book.

TOPIC B: CHORAL MUSIC

Examine both choral examples on pages 13–14 of this Question Insert.

For each example:

- Circle the appropriate school level and ensemble type on the lists in your Test Book.
- Identify and briefly describe the stylistic influences in the example, such as folk, ethnic, cultural, and/or historical characteristics.
- Identify and describe two significant performance challenges in the example. (Specify measure number(s).)
- Describe in detail appropriate rehearsal techniques to assist students in meeting each challenge.

Begin your response on page 9 of your Test Book.

TOPIC C: GENERAL MUSIC

Examine both examples on pages 15–16 of this Question Insert.

For each example:

- Circle the grade level on the list in your Test Book for which the example would be appropriate for a general music class. In your response, briefly explain your choice of grade level.
- Identify and briefly describe the stylistic influences in the example, such as folk, ethnic, cultural, and/or historical characteristics.
- Name three different musical concepts that would be most appropriately demonstrated using the example, given the grade level you have circled. Then explain in specific terms how the example could be successfully used to teach each concept.

Begin your response on page 12 of the Test Book.

NOTES

Before beginning your response, you may wish to make notes or an outline in the space provided below. Your notes will not be used in scoring your response.

-10-

QUESTION 3, TOPIC A, INSTRUMENTAL MUSIC: MUSIC SCORE NO. 1

-11-

QUESTION 3, TOPIC A, INSTRUMENTAL MUSIC: MUSICAL SCORE NO. 2

-12-

QUESTION 3, TOPIC B, CHORAL MUSIC: MUSICAL SCORE NO. 1

-13-

QUESTION 3, TOPIC B, CHORAL MUSIC: MUSICAL SCORE NO. 2

-14-

QUESTION 3, TOPIC C, GENERAL MUSIC: MUSICAL SCORE NO. 1

QUESTION 3, TOPIC C, GENERAL MUSIC: MUSICAL SCORE NO. 2

Chapter 15

Sample Responses to *Music: Analysis* and How They Were Scored

► ► ► ► ► ► ► ► ► ► ► ►

Music: Analysis Question 1

Sample Response that Earned a Score of 5

This response receives a perfect score of 5 because the test taker correctly identifies five errors. While other errors exist in the recording, the test taker is responsible for identifying only five. The test taker correctly identifies the following errors:

	Measure(s)	Error Description
1.	1	All instruments do not play beat one together
2.	21–23	Tempo accelerates
3.	5–6.	French horn does not balance to piano dynamic marking
4.	28.	Clarinet out of balance with ensemble (too loud)
5.	17–18	Clarinet places inappropriate accents on 3rd beats

Sample Response that Earned a Score of 1

This response receives a score of 1 because the test taker correctly identifies only one error. A diagnosis of each of the test taker's responses is included.

	Measure(s)	Error Description
1.	5	Bassoon dynamics - too loud on entrance
		The test taker identifies the wrong instrument as playing too loud; it is the horn, not the bassoon.
2.	17–18	Clarinet accent - misplaced count 3, should be count 2 for better phrasing.
		This is a correct response.
3.	15	Bassoon - dynamics - should be "mp" but barely audible - need to echo the play in clarinets M14 phrase
		The dynamic of the bassoon is appropriate; this is not a correct response.
4.	19	Ensemble - dynamics - performed according to markings but sounded as if the bottom dropped out - too "piano."
		The ensemble observed the markings, so there is no error.
5.	23–24	Balance - Ensemble and piano not in dynamic balance
		Incorrect—the error that should have been identified is an unwritten accelerando performed in all parts.

Music: Analysis Question 2

Sample Response that Earned a Score of 5

This response receives a perfect score of 5 because the test taker correctly identifies five errors. While other errors exist in the recording, the test taker is responsible for identifying only five. The test taker correctly identifies the following errors:

	Measure(s)	Error Description
1.	3	Altos do not perform slur (beats 2–3)
2.	9–12	Sopranos not in balance
3.	23–24	Added ritardando
4.	5–6	Tenors not in balance
5.	15–16	Ensemble does not acknowledge poco rit. marking

Sample Response that Earned a Score of 1

This response receives a score of 1 because the test taker correctly identifies only one error. A diagnosis of each of the test taker's responses is included.

	Measure(s)	Error Description
1.	M. 10	Tenors cut off early on "river" and add the word "my on the Cl (NO)
		The test taker incorrectly identifies a nonexistent error in the tenor, while missing the obvious error of the inappropriately loud soprano.
2.	M. 14	Altos extend word "river" 1 beat leaving out the word "Lord."
		The test taker incorrectly identifies a nonexistent rhythmic error.
3.	M. 20	Basses do not crescendo as marked in their part
		Incorrect—the dynamic level of the bass is appropriate.
4.	M. 21	Sopranos close vowel to `m' of pro<u>m</u>-i's'd too early (for notes G&F)
		The test taker incorrectly identifies a nonexistent diction error—and also has forgotten that diction errors are not to be identified.
5.	23–24	All parts begin a rit.
		Correct

Music: Analysis Question 3, TOPIC A: INSTRUMENTAL MUSIC

Sample Response that Earned a Score of 9

Example No. 1: (High School - Concert Band)

Stylistic influences: Baroque or Renaissance clue 4/1 polyphony (band transcription/

The test taker correctly identifies the school level and ensemble as high school concert band. The stylistic influences of Baroque and polyphony are correct, although Renaissance is not.

Performance challenge No. 1: Having the ensemble play 4/2 time having each section count and perform poly rhythm

Rehearsal technique(s) related to performance challenge No. 1: Explain 4/2 time that the 1/2 note gets the beat. Rehearse sections at a time for instance Clarinets I, II, III make sure each section counts their part. Put piece together have brass then woodwinds play separately than tutti band. Again all sections must count independently sectionals should be considered.

The test taker correctly identifies the 4/2 meter as a significant performance challenge. The test taker suggests providing an explanation of the concept and should also discuss subdivision at this point. Isolating parts is appropriate and would aid in learning the rhythm securely and in developing the students' confidence in playing contrapuntal lines.

Performance challenge No. 2: Blend and Balance intonation.

Rehearsal technique(s) related to performance challenge No. 2: The beginning of excerpt is tutti band. Rehearse section at a time making sure the students are listening to each part tell them to listen from bottom up. Even though (ff) brass should listen for woodwinds IE English horn bassoon. Balance from Bass instruments up. Make sure nice not to loud.

While the test taker correctly identifies balance as a significant performance challenge, citing several challenges or combining unrelated challenges weakens the response. The test taker should select one specific challenge and address the rehearsal techniques appropriate for that challenge. The instructions, however, to balance from the bass instruments up, keep the timbre under control, and listen to each part are appropriate rehearsal techniques to develop proper balance.

Example No. 2: (Middle/junior high - Orchestra)

Stylistic influences: Staccato unison rhythms 4 square phrasing indicated classical piece small chaimber orchestra.

The test taker correctly identifies the school level and ensemble as a middle/junior high school orchestra. Although the piece should be identified as folk-song influenced, credit is given for identifying the classical characteristic of the phrasing and string parts.

Performance challenge No. 1: Dynamics bowing staccato technique

Rehearsal technique(s) related to performance challenge No. 1: The first challenge solid (f) staccato eight note. Have the orchestra start with down-bow at the frog with bow pressure. Measure 3 rehearse piano almost subito P. Lighter bow pressure you still need nice accent on measure 4.

Although bowing and articulation could be treated separately, the test taker combines them here, along with dynamics. Probably because too many challenges were presented, the strategy described here wanders off task and falls short in adequately addressing the necessary skills to accomplish each. The attempt to explain how to achieve a solid forte is incomplete, as the test taker fails to adequately describe the degree of bow pressure to exert. The explanation of playing the piano dynamic marking in measure 3 is better, as the test taker encourages lighter bow pressure, but the reference to an "almost subito p" weakens the response as the sudden change from forte to piano should not be considered "almost subito."

Performance challenge No. 2: Even tempo intonation.

Rehearsal technique(s) related to performance challenge No. 2: Carefully rehearse large interval skip—measure 34, 7–11, 12

Tempo - Establish good steady moderato tempo having students sub-divide orally or by clapping eighth and sixteenth note 1 & 2 & then have violin viola cello clap the rhythm of excerpt. Once students can sub divide - have them play the song even tempo important.

The test taker correctly identifies two performance challenges: an even tempo and intonation. The rhythm pattern of the eighth-sixteenth-sixteenth figure could pose difficulties as students may either rush or drag this figure. The intonation of the parallel unison passages, especially the skip of the seventh, may be a challenge. Because both challenges occur simultaneously in specific measures, the test taker chooses to combine the challenges, although he or she could have focused on just one with more success. The test taker briefly addresses the intonation of the large interval skip. While "careful" rehearsing of particular measures would be a good start, the test taker should be more specific as to how this should be accomplished, such as including a description of slow practice while tuning within and among sections with different combinations of instruments. The test taker addresses the concept of tempo better. By subdividing orally or clapping, the correct rhythm can be reinforced.

Overall, the response does not receive a perfect score because of the weaknesses discussed, but it still receives a high score.

Sample Response that Earned a Score of 6

Example No. 1: (high school - concert band)

Stylistic influences: Mahler for broad brass sound with woodwind melody?

The test taker correctly identifies the school level and ensemble as high school concert band. However, the stylistic influences are incorrectly identified. This work is by Bach, from the Baroque period and transcribed for band; it is not a piece from the late Romantic by Mahler.

Performance challenge No. 1: tuning accidentals

Rehearsal technique(s) related to performance challenge No. 1: Play slowly listening and correcting pitch as sections or close sections. Acknowledge harmonic changes and leading tones.

It seems unlikely that a high school concert band that is ready to take on this piece would have particular difficulties tuning accidentals. If, however, the test takers had described an appropriate technique addressing that challenge, some credit could have been given. Unfortunately, the strategy described here is too vague. Playing "slowly, listening and correcting pitch" would only be an initial step in addressing the challenge. Further discussion, such as tuning between and among the sections while building chords from the bass instruments up, is necessary.

Performance challenge No. 2: Rhythmic definition of eight notes m. 2 & 4. while maintain smooth articulation and sustained ?????

Rehearsal technique(s) related to performance challenge No. 2: Clap and say rhythm together. Subdivide and lave them play together w/out group. Play separated eight to hear ??? then play ???? to hear difference.

The eighth notes specifically are not a significant performance challenge for a high school concert band. The test taker could have identified the moving lines of the inner parts as the significant performance challenge instead. Focusing only on the eighth notes demonstrates that the test taker is unaware of the important issue. The strategy, however, would help to address the rhythm challenge presented. Clapping, isolating parts, subdividing, and comparing performances are all appropriate techniques in addressing rhythm challenges.

Example No. 2: (middle/junior high - orchestra)

Stylistic influences: Beethoven and Hyden for consistent rhythmic themes and form, and unison.

The test taker correctly identifies the school level and ensemble as a middle/junior high orchestra. The piece is a folk song, but because the test taker identified classical rhythmical elements, credit can be given. The test taker should use appropriate musical terms. Also, a stronger answer would have been to identify the stylistic influences as classical, rather than specifying two composers.

Performance challenge No. 1: rhythmic uniformity with out rushing the piece. Keeping stacc. eights distinctively different from non stacc. w/o rushing.

Rehearsal technique(s) related to performance challenge No. 1: Clap & say rhythm together. Subdivide and have them play together w/out group. Play separate eighths to hear beat. Then play connected to hear difference.

The test taker correctly identifies the rhythm and articulation as a significant performance challenge. The test taker presents appropriate rehearsal techniques of clapping and chanting the rhythm, apparently in sections and as an entire ensemble, and isolating the articulation styles.

Performance challenge No. 2: Uniform bow changes allowing for easier and best articulation.

Rehearsal technique(s) related to performance challenge No. 2: Have parts marked with bowings which would be different then how it comes. ex. meas. 2 would be V V ⊓ to aid in the accent of beat 2. Then retake to measure 3 slowly go through the piece making sure all markings are in. Practice accented notes with a down bow and up bow. Practice stacc. notes with down bow and up bow.

The test taker correctly identifies a significant performance challenge as bowings. The description of the rehearsal technique demonstrates the test taker's knowledge of bowing techniques and strategies to achieve this. The response could have been strengthened by explaining how the distinction between the techniques of accenting and playing staccato would be clarified for the students.

Sample Response that Earned a Score of 2

Example No. 1: (high school - orchestra)

Stylistic influences: Classical—pretty straight forward.

The test taker incorrectly identifies the ensemble as an orchestra, although no string parts are evident in the score. The stylistic influences are incorrectly identified as classical.

Performance challenge No. 1: Time signature of 4/2

Rehearsal technique(s) related to performance challenge No. 1: Get students used to playing in 4/2. Before playing, clap rhythm in parts then altogether. Have students write rhythm counts on their sheet music.

The test taker correctly identifies a significant performance challenge. The rehearsal technique, however, is inadequate to prepare students for playing in this meter, so no credit was given for the rehearsal technique. An appropriate strategy would include an explanation of the concepts of 4/2 meter and subdivision. Writing counts on sheet music is an ineffective strategy.

Performance challenge No. 2: Holding notes

Rehearsal technique(s) related to performance challenge No. 2: Some may have trouble holding notes at ff, so we'll rehearse efficient breathing – deep, controlled.

Both the challenge and the rehearsal technique are too vague and laconic. "Holding notes" could refer simply to the whole notes and tied notes, which does not constitute a significant performance challenge for a high school band. The rehearsal technique is little more than a restatement of the challenge, from which one can surmise that the test taker is after breath control. The test taker could have explained how maintaining the proper breath support for the long phrases might be rehearsed. This could have been a strong answer had more detail been provided.

Example No. 2: (middel/junior high concert band)

Stylistic influences: String ensemble w/ piano accomp, very simple, straight forward Baroque/Classical.

The test taker incorrectly identifies the ensemble as a concert band then mentions a string ensemble with piano accompaniment, indicating a lack of understanding of ensemble instrumentation. The descriptive words "simple, straightforward" do not illuminate the test taker's understanding of stylistic influences. Further damage is done by mentioning both Baroque and Classical as if the two styles were equivalent.

Performance challenge No. 1: string bass playing slightly different rhythm (mm. 3–4, 7, 11–12, 15)

Rehearsal technique(s) related to performance challenge No. 1: Clap rhythm together getting string bass used to the rests when everyone else is playing.

The test taker incorrectly identifies the rhythm of the string bass as presenting a significant performance challenge. The bass part is only a simplification (with omission of the two sixteenth notes) of the other parts. Were this a significant challenge, the rehearsal technique of clapping the appropriate rhythm would necessitate isolation of the bass part, not clapping the rhythm "altogether" as the test taker suggests.

Performance challenge No. 2: playing with piano accomp

Rehearsal technique(s) related to performance challenge No. 2: string ensemble have their parts down before adding piano accomp so that they are secure in their parts (especially rhythmically). In my experiences, students have the most difficulty with rhythm.

It is more likely that the piano accompaniment would provide a rhythmic basis for the ensemble, reinforcing a steady beat, and would make the rhythms easier to perform. The test taker does not describe a rehearsal technique. Stating that "they are secure in their parts" does not address the process of adding a difficult accompaniment, if such were the case. The test taker's response indicates little ability to analyze performance challenges or provide appropriate rehearsal techniques. No credit was given for the performance challenge or the rehearsal technique.

Music: Analysis Question 3, TOPIC B: CHORAL MUSIC

Sample Response that Earned a Score of 10

Example No. 1: (high school - madrigal/chamber choir)

Stylistic influences: A madrigal piece from the renaissance maybe Morley

The test taker correctly identifies the school level and ensemble type as a high school madrigal/chamber choir. The style is correctly identified as that of a madrigal from the Renaissance by Morley.

Performance challenge No. 1: Rhythm through the fa la la section each part singing different rhythms.

Rehearsal technique(s) related to performance challenge No. 1: Get in groups by section rehearse each section saying only Fa la la singing at a slow tempo. Put all groups together & just speak the words in rhythm. Have section leader point out problems. They learn the notes - each part separately and put it together with all four parts. Rehearse Sop I & II together Bottom 3 part together if necessary.

The test taker correctly identifies a performance challenge. Chanting the words in rhythm at a slower tempo in sections separately prior to singing the notes, and finally putting the sections together, is an appropriately sequenced rehearsal technique.

Performance challenge No. 2: Quick dynamic changes. Drastic change with no crescendo.

Rehearsal technique(s) related to performance challenge No. 2: Do scales & warmups watching director. Change conduction style quickly forcing students to be on their toes & watching at all times. Rehearse the piece & conduct the same way. Also practice keeping energy & support through soft sections.

The dynamics as written may pose a performance challenge. Practicing changes in dynamics with a conductor is a common technique and would probably be helpful in this case. This piece should be light and buoyant in the fa-la-la section, so the test taker's suggestion to maintain energy and support throughout is appropriate.

Example No. 2: (high school – mixed choir)

Stylistic influences: rhythm & lyrics suggest a folk influence

The test taker correctly identifies the school level and ensemble type as junior high mixed choir. The stylistic influences of folk rhythm and lyrics are correct.

Performance challenge No. 1: Rhythm measure 7. 3rd time singing these lyrics the rhythm changes & sops have different rhythm than other 2 parts

The test taker correctly identifies a significant performance challenge. The change of the rhythm in measure 7 is the third repetition of the word, "River," reversing the order of the eighth and dotted-quarter notes of the previous two times. In this case, Part I holds the note while the other two parts change on the beat.

Rehearsal technique(s) related to performance challenge No. 1: count & clap measure one with whole group. Count & clap measure 7 Alto & Bari together & sops alone. Count & clap measure 7 altogether. Alternate clapping measure 1 & 7 a few times. Say the words in rhythm for the whole piece giving them a heads up on measure 7

Counting and clapping the rhythm changes between measure 1 and measure 7 is an appropriate rehearsal technique. Isolating Part I from the other parts will help with mastery.

Performance challenge No. 2: brief change in tonality in measure 5 & 6 mostly altos

The test taker correctly identifies a significant performance challenge: the chromaticism leading to a brief change in tonality in measures 5 and 6.

Rehearsal technique(s) related to performance challenge No. 2: sing on solfege altering so to si & back to so in measure 6. Altos only sing with the piano measure 5 & 6 to better hear complete tonality change. Sing solfege with all parts listening carefully to the altos. Add words & piano accompaniment to help out — All parts

The test taker describes an appropriate rehearsal technique to meet the performance challenge. Isolating Part II with the piano, and then with all parts, allows that part to be heard in the sonority of the chord.

Sample Response that Earned a Score of 4

Example No. 1: (high school)

Stylistic influences: Folk song, talk about message in song. Is it a love song, or a real fire.

The test taker correctly identifies the school level as high school but fails to indicate the ensemble type. The test taker fails to recognize the stylistic influences of a Renaissance madrigal.

Performance challenge No. 1: mixed meters measures 7–12.

The test taker correctly identifies the meter changes as a significant performance challenge.

Rehearsal technique(s) related to performance challenge No. 1: have them clap out the mixed meter slowly after director demonstrates then chant in monotone, then go over.

The response is only partially correct. A more detailed description of the rehearsal technique would show greater understanding: clapping out the mixed meter would be more effective if students were counting quarter-note pulses as they shifted between meters. Modeling by the director, followed by chanting, is appropriate. Chanting in a monotone is not effective; the natural inflection of the words would contribute to rhythmic understanding.

Performance challenge No. 2: All parts not in unison rhythm.

The description of the performance challenge is rather vague. A high school choir should not find "rhythms not in unison" a significant performance challenge. The challenge is the polyphonic nature of the piece. A stronger response would use the appropriate musical term and identify the sections that are especially challenging, such as the fa-la-la section, but this answer still receives credit.

Rehearsal technique(s) related to performance challenge No. 2: Have sectionals if not possible to separate do it in the group one section at a time, phrase by phrase. Clap out rhythmic problem areas. Rehearse slowly. Demonstrate difficult parts.

Addressing the sections individually is an appropriate first step, but the test taker's intention of "phrase by phrase, clap out rhythmic problem areas" is expressed too vaguely and fails to address the challenge of combining the different rhythms of each section simultaneously, which is the performance challenge identified above.

Example No. 2: middle/junior high

Stylistic influences: spiritual, contemplating, not fast

The test taker correctly identifies the school level as middle/junior high but fails to indicate the ensemble type. The stylistic influence is not correctly identified. The lyrics are not indicative of a spiritual but rather of a folk song.

Performance challenge No. 1: syncopation mes. 1, 3, 5, 7

The test taker correctly identifies the eighth note followed by a dotted quarter note as syncopation in measures 1 and 3 but incorrectly includes measures 5 and 7. Because the test taker's understanding of the musical term and ability to perceive it in the music is incorrect, the response did not receive credit.

Rehearsal technique(s) related to performance challenge No. 1: hand clap mes 1–2, 3–4, 5–6, 7–8 Than sing in monotone voice

Clapping and chanting the rhythm is an appropriate technique, but, as stated earlier, singing in a monotone voice is not. The test taker should complete the sequence by having the students sing the correct pitches to the rhythms, and then rehearse the complete phrases. This answer is vague and incomplete but receives credit.

Performance challenge No. 2: articulation in part II mes 4, 4, 6, 7

The phrasing of these measures could be considered a performance challenge, but the articulation style is not.

Rehearsal technique(s) related to performance challenge No. 2: Explain what a two note slur is. Demonstrate technique.

This answer is too general to receive credit. Any performance challenge should be explained and demonstrated. Specific rehearsal techniques should directly address the performance challenge.

Sample Response that Earned a Score of 2

Example No. 1: (high school, madrigal/chamber choir)

Stylistic influences: this is probably written Morley – Renaissance period

Performance challenge No. 1: would give the student the students their parts and see if they can sightread it

Rehearsal technique(s) related to performance challenge No. 1: First we would observe the time signature thru-out the music, attempt to beat the rhythm. I would play their parts out for them to hear and play their parts out as they attempt to sing it.

Performance challenge No. 2: After they have practiced it a few times with the piano, then they would be requested to sing it accappella.

Rehearsal technique(s) related to performance challenge No. 2: [blank]

Example No. 2: (middle/junior high)

Stylistic influences: maybe 3 part music -- folk song

Performance challenge No. 1: see if students can sight read the song with the rhythm

Rehearsal technique(s) related to performance challenge No. 1: Practice singing parts with the solfege, each section would sing their part, observe dynamics and breathing techniques.

Performance challenge No. 2: Final preparation would include playing the accompaniment

Rehearsal technique(s) related to performance challenge No. 2: [blank]

For both examples, the test taker correctly identifies the stylistic influences. On the other hand, the response consistently fails to respond to the tasks posed and does not identify any performance challenges or rehearsal techniques. Instead, a generic rehearsal plan is provided, demonstrating no understanding of possible performance challenges and rehearsal techniques.

Music: Analysis Question 3, TOPIC C: GENERAL MUSIC

Sample Response that Earned a Score of 9

Example No. 1

Grade level: 4–5

Defense of grade-level selection: All of the steps of the scale are present including "fa" and "ti". In addition, the rhythm ♩. ♪ is a rhythmic concept that is typically presented at this grade level.

Stylistic influences: This music is influenced by folk music, in particular English folk songs. This can be sung as a three part round.

The test taker correctly identifies the grade level as 4–5 and provides an acceptable rationale. The stylistic influences of an English round song are correctly identified.

First concept: 3-Part Round

How the piece could be used to teach that concept: The chords for each line are the same. The students would first be taught the whole piece by rote then sung in two part round. First the students sing then the teacher sings a round with them. Then the class can be divided into two groups. The class will then sing a two part round (the teacher cues in groups), and when they are ready they can go on to singing in 3 parts w/the teacher, then divide class.

The first concept of introducing a three-part round is correctly identified and developed appropriately. This experience could be used to introduce students to polyphonic texture.

Second concept: Rhythmic concept ♩. ♪.

How the piece could be used to teach that concept: No other unknown rhythm is present in the piece. Have the children first dictate the rhythms of the first two lines as this would be prior knowledge, then fill in the known rhythms on the last line. The children should have already sung several songs with this rhythm and be prepared for this presentation of ♩. ♪. Have them listen to how many sounds on each beat then find any ties. Teach first as ♩. ♪.

The introduction of the dotted rhythm is an appropriate concept. Elements of the overall development of the concept are acceptable, but the steps are not sequenced properly to ensure the transfer of understanding from the tied version to the dotted notation.

Third concept: Steps and skips

How the piece could be used to teach that concept: This piece contains descending lines in step and skips.

A more appropriate concept for 4–5 grade would have been the identification of intervals of seconds and thirds, or an introduction of the diatonic scale or major scale, which descends in phrase 1 and ascends in phrase 2. Concepts of melodic contour, phrases, and sequence could also have been developed. The explanation of how the piece could be used to teach the concept of steps and skips is merely a restatement of the concept; more detail is needed to receive complete credit.

Example No. 2

Grade level: 4–5

Defense of grade-level selection: This piece contains the rhythm ♪♩♪.

Stylistic influences: African music.

The test taker correctly identifies the grade level as 4–5 and provides an appropriate defense. The test taker fails to recognize the text, pentatonic mode, and repeated melodic and rhythmic content as Native American.

First concept: ♪♩♪.

How the piece could be used to teach that concept: This piece contains ♪♩♪ which would be the only unknown rhythmic element in this piece. The students should have already sung other songs w/this rhythm. Dictation of all other rhythms then present the new rhythm.

While the dictation of the other rhythms provides an opportunity for review, the test taker could have focused more on explaining the presentation of a new concept related to the rhythm. More detail is needed than merely, "present the new rhythm." This answer receives only partial credit.

Second concept: Ethnic Music

How the piece could be used to teach that concept: This piece is African in style and the students can study the country of origin and the typical elements of the music. Including syncopation.

The second concept of "Ethnic Music" is too vague to serve as an appropriate concept. On the other hand, the idea of discussing stylistic aspects of a culture's music from the perspective of how musical elements—melody, rhythm, form, harmony, timbre, texture, and so on—are treated is appropriate. Syncopation is an appropriate rhythmical concept.

Third concept: ♫♩♫ same sound more notes

How the piece could be used to teach that concept: Wee ♫♩♫ on one sound.

The third concept of three slurred eighth notes is appropriate but is not accurately described. The explanation of how the example could be used to teach this concept is only a restatement of the concept.

Sample Response that Earned a Score of 5

Example No. 1

Grade level: 2–3

Defense of grade-level selection: This piece is simple enough in its rhythm and pitch intervals for any grade level, but the voice range goes a little high for kindergarteners or first grades—who also might have trouble with a word like whither. The cut time might also prove a little tricky for them. It also has a major sixth interval which might also be challenging for the very young.

Stylistic influences: This is basically an old English folk song, probably from the 1800's or even 1700's judging from its use of the words "whither" and "greenwood."

The test taker selects too low a grade level. The wide vocal range and the indication that this can be sung as a round suggests an older grade level of 4–5 or 6–8. The test taker correctly identifies, however, the stylistic influences of an English folk song.

First concept: English folk songs

How the piece could be used to teach that concept: This song could exemplify a piece of English folk song music and could be part of a broader lesson on English/Irish folk song music that included pieces like "Shenandoah" or "My Bonnie Lies Over the Ocean."

"English folk songs" is too broad to stand as an appropriate musical concept. Comparing the use of musical elements between different songs would be appropriate, but the response is too vague in what and how concepts will be taught.

Second concept: Teaching rhythm-progressively more complex

How the piece could be used to teach that concept: The first line of the song could be used to identify 1/2 and whole notes. The second line could be used to teach eighth notes in addition to the half and whole note. Finally, dotted rhythms could be added in the third line.

The second concept of teaching various rhythms is appropriate and sequenced correctly but was not explained clearly.

Third concept: The notes of the major scale.

How the piece could be used to teach that concept: This piece uses all the notes of the C major scale. The lesson could begin by having the kids sing do-re-mi-fa-sol-la-ti-do in C and then sing the song. They could also label the notes of the song in terms of what scale role they are in the C scale. (1–7 or do–ti).

The test taker correctly identifies the third concept of introducing the major scale and provides a specific explanation of how the piece can be used to teach this by suggesting singing solfège and labeling the notes of the song.

Example No. 2

Grade Level: K–1

Defense of grade-level selection: This is a relatively simple song with a small and low enough pitch range for any age. None of the intervals are large and it has an easy to follow flow to it despite being somewhat exotic in style.

Stylistic influences: It seems to be a Native American folk song of some sort judging from the notes and words of the song and chant-like rhythm and overall quality.

Although the test taker provides a defense for selecting the grade level of K–1, this song is more appropriate for older elementary grades. The test taker correctly identifies some stylistic influences of Native American folk songs.

First concept: This could be part of a lesson in Native American music/culture.

How the piece could be used to teach that concept: This is an example of Native American music. We could note the chant-like pitches and rhythms that are typical of that music.

Second concept: Alternative rhythms.

Third concept: Other language.

Example No. 2

The first concept the test taker addresses is not a musical concept. The test taker should consider selecting concepts from the elements of music: melody, rhythm, form, harmony, timbre, and texture. The explanations of the second and third concepts are incomplete, and receive no credit.

Sample Response that Earned a Score of 3

Example No. 1

Grade Level: 2–3

Defense of grade-level selection: Children in grade levels 2-3 could learn the repetition of the words easier than more complex lyrics. Only a melody is sung without other parts to make it more confusing for the younger student. Its also short less words to remember. The progression of the notes in the beginning makes it easier to sing.

Stylistic influences: This piece has a folk or religious style to it, the "with spirit" dynamics indicates a spiritual feeling and the words indicate an older more folk type song. Cut time is often seen in folk music as well.

The test taker selects too low a grade level. The wide vocal range and the indication that this can be sung as a round suggests an older grade level of 4–5 or 6–8. The test taker seems confused by the tempo marking, "with spirit," and fails to identify the stylistic influences as an English round song.

First concept: timing

How the piece could be used to teach that concept: This would be a good piece to teach cut time. Many children understand 4/4 timing and have been introduced to it, but not to cut time.

The first concept of introducing cut time is appropriate. The test taker does not identify cut time at first, revealing what is meant by "timing" in the explanation that follows, but fails to explain how to use this example to teach this concept. Only partial credit can be given here.

Second concept: to sing a variety of notes.

How the piece could be used to teach that concept: The piece begins simple and gets more complex as it progresses. it also has a variety of note changes that go up and down the scale and also some changing in steps to give practice for singing those notes. only one measure has a large jump from a lower note to a high one, which gives another skill rather than all notes being close together.

The second concept is not correctly identified. The test taker's idea is too broad to receive credit.

Third concept: Teaching about the idea of chords.

How the piece could be used to teach that concept: The chords written above the piece indicate the chords in the music. This could be discussed with students as a beginning concept that chords do exist and are used in songs and their importance.

The third concept of teaching chords is appropriate, but the explanation could have been more specific. The test taker suggests a discussion about the chords but should have indicated what that would entail. Only partial credit can be given here.

Example No. 2

Grade Level: K–1

Defense of grade-level selection: This age group would like this song for the fun and the silly words. The timing is basic and the "words" simple.

Stylistic influences: It will sound like a chant to a child like Native American music style.

This song is more appropriate for older elementary grades. The test taker correctly identifies the stylistic influences of Native American music.

First concept: Rhythm

How the piece could be used to teach that concept: This is a good song for some fun exercises in rhythm without have to concentrate to heavy on lyrics you can teach the rhythm of the song.

Second concept: Singing the appropriate notes.

How the piece could be used to teach that concept: Many young students don't recognize the changes in the pitch this level help to get the students to listen to the notes and "match" their voices to them. Then range of notes is small and not too high.

The first and second concepts the test taker suggests are too vague to receive credit.

Third concept: Key signature

How the piece could be used to teach that concept: A good piece to point out that a key signature does exist and a time to talk about sharps and flats not in great detail just what they look like and that the black keys on a piano are the sharps and flats you see here written on the page.

The third concept is too advanced for the grade level the test taker selected—K–1. This concept would be more appropriate for older elementary grades. No credit was given.

Chapter 16

Are You Ready? Last-Minute Tips

► ► ► ► ► ► ► ► ► ► ► ►

Checklist

Complete this checklist to determine whether you're ready to take the test.

- ❏ Do you know the testing requirements for your teaching field in the state(s) where you plan to teach?
- ❏ Have you followed all of the test registration procedures?
- ❏ Do you know the topics that will be covered in each test you plan to take?
- ❏ Have you reviewed any textbooks, class notes, musical pieces, and course readings that relate to the topics covered?
- ❏ Do you know how long the test will take and the number of questions it contains? Have you considered how you will pace your work?
- ❏ Are you familiar with the test directions and the types of questions on the test?
- ❏ Are you familiar with the recommended test-taking strategies and tips?
- ❏ Have you worked through the practice test questions at a pace similar to that of an actual test?
- ❏ If you are repeating a Praxis Series™ Assessment, have you analyzed your previous score report to determine areas where additional study and test preparation could be useful?

The Day of the Test

You should have ended your review a day or two before the actual test date. And many clichés you may have heard about the day of the test are true. You should

- Be well rested
- Take photo identification with you
- Take a supply of well-sharpened #2 pencils (at least three) if you are taking the multiple-choice test
- Take blue or black ink pens if you are taking a constructed-response test
- Take your admission ticket, letter of authorization, mailgram, or telegram with you
- Eat before you take the test, and take some food or a snack to keep your energy level up
- Wear layered clothing; room temperature may vary
- Be prepared to stand in line to check in or to wait while other test takers are being checked in

You can't control the testing situation, but you can control yourself. Stay calm. The supervisors are well trained and make every effort to provide uniform testing conditions, but don't let it bother you if the test doesn't start exactly on time. You will have the necessary amount of time once it does start.

You can think of preparing for this test as training for an athletic event. Once you've trained, prepared, and rested, give it everything you've got. Good luck.

Appendix A
Study Plan Sheet

Study Plan Sheet

See chapter 1 for suggestions on using this Study Plan Sheet.

STUDY PLAN

Content covered on test	How well do I know the content?	What material do I have for studying this content?	What material do I need for studying this content?	Where could I find the materials I need?	Dates planned for study of content	Dates completed

Appendix B

For More Information

► ► ► ► ► ► ► ► ► ► ► ►

Educational Testing Service offers additional information to assist you in preparing for the Praxis Series™ Assessments. *Tests at a Glance* materials and the *Registration Bulletin* are both available without charge (see below to order). You can also obtain more information from our Web site: www.ets.org/praxis/index.html.org.

General Inquires

Phone: 609-771-7395 (Monday-Friday, 8:00 a.m. to 8:00 p.m., Eastern time)
Fax: 609-771-7906

Extended Time

If you have a learning disability or if English is not your primary language, you can apply to be given more time to take your test. The *Registration Bulletin* tells you how you can qualify for extended time.

Disability Services

Phone: 609-771-7780
Fax: 609-771-7906
TTY (for deaf or hard-of-hearing callers): 609-771-7714

Mailing Address

Praxis
Educational Testing Service
P.O. Box 6051
Princeton, NJ 08541-6051

Overnight Delivery Address

Praxis
Educational Testing Service
Distribution Center
225 Phillips Blvd.
P.O. Box 77435
Ewing, NJ 08628-7435

Appendix C
Index Numbers on the Enclosed CD

► ► ► ► ► ► ► ► ► ► ► ►

Index Numbers on the Enclosed CD

Content Knowledge Practice Test

[1] Directions for the recorded section
and Music for Question 1

[2]–[27] Music for Questions 2–27

Analysis Practice Test

[28] Directions for the recorded section

[29] Music for Question 1

[30] Music for Question 2

Appendix D
List of Resources

This is intended as neither an exhaustive compilation nor an endorsement of these particular texts or the approaches they represent. It is included as a helpful starting place for study. Many other texts may also prove useful.

Since new editions are constantly being introduced into the market, the citations below were intentionally generalized to exclude particular publication dates and specific editions. Look for the most recent edition of any text you use for studying.

Music History

Grout, Donald J., and Claude Palisca. *A History of Western Music.* W. W. Norton.

Kamien, Roger. *Music: An Appreciation.* McGraw-Hill.

Kirchner, Bill, ed. *The Oxford Companion to Jazz.* Oxford University Press.

Machlis, Joseph, and Kristine Forney. *The Enjoyment of Music.* W. W. Norton.

Megill, Donald D., and Richard S. Demory. *Introduction to Jazz History.* Prentice-Hall/Simon & Schuster.

Miller, Hugh H., and Dale Cockrell. *History of Western Music.* HarperPerennial.

Sadie, Stanley, and John Tyrrell, eds. *The New Grove Dictionary of Music and Musicians.* Oxford University Press.

Slonimsky, Nicholas, and Laura Kuhn, eds. *Baker's Biographical Dictionary of Musicians.* Schirmer.

Music Theory

Burkhart, Charles. *Anthology for Musical Analysis.* Harcourt Brace College Publishers.

Jones, George Thaddeus. *Music Theory.* Barnes & Noble Books.

Ottman, Robert W. *Elementary Harmony: Theory and Practice.* Prentice-Hall.

Ottman, Robert W. *Advanced Harmony: Theory and Practice.* Prentice-Hall.

Lerner-Sexton, Marie. *AP Music Theory Teacher's Guide.* The College Board.

Conducting and Orchestration

Burton, Stephen. *Orchestration.* Prentice-Hall.

Garretson, Robert L. *Conducting Choral Music.* Prentice-Hall.

Green, Elizabeth. *The Modern Conductor.* Prentice Hall.

Hunsberger, Donald, and Roy Ernst. *The Art of Conducting.* McGraw-Hill.

McElleran, Brock. *Conducting Technique.* Oxford University Press.

Philosophy of Music Education

Elliott, David. *Music Matters: A New Philosophy of Music Education.* Oxford University Press.

Reimer, Bennett. *A Philosophy of Music Education: Advancing the Vision.* Prentice-Hall.

Music Education Research

Colwell, Richard, and Carol E. Richardson, eds. *The New Handbook of Research on Music Teaching and Learning*. Oxford University Press.

Price, Harry, ed. *Music Education Research: An Anthology from the Journal of Research in Music Education.* MENC—The National Association for Music Education.

History of American Music Education

Mark, Michael L., and Charles E. Gary. *A History of American Music Education.* MENC—The National Association for Music Education.

Psychology of Music

Boyle, J. David, and Rudolf E. Radocy. *Psychological Foundations of Musical Behavior*. Charles C. Thomas Publisher.

Hargreaves, David J. *The Developmental Psychology of Music*. Cambridge University Press.

Classroom Management

MENC—The National Association for Music Education. *Classroom Management in General, Choral, and Instrumental Music Programs.*

Moore, Marvelene C., Angela L. Batey, and David M. Royse. *Classroom Management in General, Choral, and Instrumental Music Programs*. MENC—The National Association for Music Education.

Technology

MENC—The National Association for Music Education. *Opportunity-to-Learn Standards for Music Technology*. Available at www.menc.org/.

MENC—The National Association for Music Education. *Strategies for Teaching Technology.*

Williams, D. B., and P. R. Webster, *Experiencing Music Technology.* Wadsworth.

Ethics

American Federation of Musicians, et al. *The Music Code of Ethics*. MENC—The National Association for Music Education. Available at www.menc.org/.

Foundations of Music Education

Abeles, H., C. Hoffer, and R. Klotman. *Foundations of Music Education*. Schirmer.

Bigge, M., et al. *Learning Theories for Teachers*. Addison Wesley.

Bluestine, Eric. *The Ways Children Learn Music*. GIA.

Gordon, Edwin E. *Learning Sequences in Music*. GIA.

Hackett, Patricia, and Carolyn A. Lindeman.*The Musical Classroom: Backgrounds, models and skills for elementary teaching*. Prentice Hall.

Labuta, Joseph A., and Deborah A. Smith. *Music Education: Historical contexts and perspectives.* Prentice Hall.

Lefrancois, G. *Psychology for Teaching*. Wadsworth.

Mark, Michael L. *Contemporary Music Education*. Schirmer Books.

Nettl, B., et al. *Excursions in World Music*. Pearson.

Stokes, M., et al. *Ethnicity, Identity, and Music: The Musical Construction of Place*. Berg.

Titon, J. T., et al. *Worlds of Music*. Wadsworth.

Walker, D. E. *Teaching Music: Managing the Successful Music Program*. Schirmer.

Zimmerman, M. *The Musical Characteristics of Children*. MENC—The National Association for Music Education.

Band/Orchestra

Colwell, Richard, and Thomas Goolsby. *The Teaching of Instrumental Music*. Prentice-Hall.

Cook, Gary. *Teaching Percussion*. Schirmer Books/Wadsworth Publishing Company.

Holloway, Ronald A., and Harry R. Bartlett. *Guide to Teaching Percussion*. Wm. C. Brown.

Hunt, Norman J. *Guide to Teaching Brass*. Wm. C. Brown.

Klotman, Robert. *Teaching Strings: Technique and Pedagogy*. Schirmer Books/Wadsworth Publishing Company.

Lamb, Norman. *Guide to Teaching Strings*. Wm. C. Brown.

Littrell, David, et al. *Teaching Music through Performance in Orchestra*. GIA.

MENC—The National Association for Music Education. *Teaching Stringed Instruments: A Course of Study*.

Miles, Richard, et al. *Teaching Music through Performance in Band* (4 vol.). GIA.

Schleuter, Stanley L. *A Sound Approach to Teaching Instrumentalists*. Schirmer Books/Wadsworth Publishing Company.

Westphal, Frederick. *Guide to Teaching Woodwinds*. Wm. C. Brown.

[see also *Strategies for Teaching* series, under "Standards and Assessment"]

Chorus

Collins, Donald L. *Teaching Choral Music*. Prentice-Hall.

Garretson, Robert L. *Choral Music: History, Style, and Performance Practice*. Prentice-Hall.

May, William V., and Craig Tolin. *Pronunciation Guide for Choral Literature*. MENC—The National Association for Music Education.

Miller, K. *Vocal Music Education*. Prentice Hall.

MENC—The National Association for Music Education. *Teaching Choral Music: A Course of Study*.

MENC—The National Association for Music Education. *Spotlight on Teaching Chorus*.

Winold, A., and R. Robinson. *Choral Experience: Literature, Materials, and Methods*. Waveland Press.

[see also *Strategies for Teaching* series, under "Standards and Assessment"]

General Music

Anderson, William M., and Joy E. Lawrence. *Integrating Music into the Classroom*. Wadsworth Publishing Company.

Anderson, William A., and Patricia Shehan Campbell, eds. *Multicultural Perspectives in Music Education*. MENC—The National Association for Music Education.

Campbell, Patricia Shehan, and Carol Scott-Kassner. *Music in Childhood: From Preschool through the Elementary Grades*. Wadsworth Publishing Company.

Fowler, Charles. *Music! Its Role and Importance in Our Lives*. Glencoe/McGraw-Hill.

Hackett, Patricia, and Carolynn A. Lindeman. *The Musical Classroom: Backgrounds, Models, and Skills for Elementary Teaching*. Prentice-Hall.

MENC—The National Association for Music Education. *Teaching General Music: A Course of Study*.

Rozmajzl, Michon, and Rene Boyer-White. *Music Fundamentals, Methods and Materials for the Elementary Classroom Teacher*. Longman Publishing Group.

Titon, Jeff Todd, ed. *Worlds of Music: An Introduction to the Music of the World's Peoples*. Wadsworth Publishing Company.

[see also *Strategies for Teaching* series, under "Standards and Assessment"]

Other Music Education

Abeles, Harold F., Charles R. Hoffer, and Robert H. Klotman. *Foundations of Music Education*. Schirmer Books/Wadsworth Publishing Company.

Barrett, Janet R., Claire W. McCoy, and Kati K. Veblen. *Sound Ways of Knowing: Music in the Interdisciplinary Curriculum*. Schirmer Books/Wadsworth Publishing Company.

Boardman, Eunice, ed. *Dimensions of Musical Learning and Teaching: A Different Kind of Classroom.* MENC—The National Association for Music Education.

Choksy, Lois, Robert M. Abramson, Avon E. Gillespie, David Woods, and Frank York. *Teaching Music in the Twenty-first Century*. Prentice-Hall.

Hoffer, Charles R. *Introduction to Music Education*. Waveland Press.

Hoffer, Charles R. *Teaching Music in the Secondary Schools*. Wadsworth Publishing Company.

Kaplan, Phyllis R., and Sandra L. Stauffer. *Cooperative Learning in Music*. MENC—The National Association for Music Education.

Lindeman, Carolynn A. *PianoLab: An Introduction to Class Piano*. Thomson Learning/Schirmer.

Mark, Michael L. *Contemporary Music Education*. Schirmer Books/Wadsworth Publishing Company.

MENC—The National Association for Music Education. *Integrating Music and Reading Instruction*.

Rudophy, Tom E. *Teaching Music with Technology*. GIA Publications.

Walker, Darwin E. *Teaching Music: Managing the Successful Music Program*. Schirmer Books/Wadsworth Publishing Company.

Music Approaches (Orff, Kodaly, etc.)

Carder, Polly, ed. *The Eclectic Curriculum in American Music Education*. MENC—The National Association for Music Education.

Choksy, Lois. *The Kodaly Method I: Comprehensive Music Education*. Prentice-Hall.

Frazee, Jane, and Kent Krewter. *Discovering Orff: A Curriculum for Music Teachers*. Warner Bros. Publications.

Gordon, Edwin. *Learning Sequences in Music: Skill, Content, and Patterns*. GIA Publications.

Jaques-Dalcroze, Emile. *Rhythm, Music and Education*. Trans. H. F. Rubenstein. The Dalcroze Society.

Saliba, Konnie K. *Accent on Orff: An Introductory Approach*. Prentice-Hall.

Special Learners

Greenspan, S., et. al. *The Child With Special Needs*. Perseus.

Schaberg, Gail. *TIPS: Teaching Music to Special Learners*. MENC—The National Association for Music Education.

Sobol, Elise S. *An Attitude and Approach for Teaching Music to Special Learners*. Pentland Press/MENC—The National Association for Music Education.

Standards and Assessment

Boyle, D., and R. Radocy. *Measurement and Evaluation of Musical Experiences*. Schirmer.

Brophy, Timothy S. *Assessing the Developing Child Musician: A Guide for General Music Teachers*. GIA Publications.

Consortium of National Arts Education Associations. *National Standards for Arts Education: What Every Young American Should Know and Be Able to Do in the Arts*. MENC—The National Association for Music Education.

Cutietta, Robert A., ed. *Strategies for Teaching Specialized Ensembles*. MENC—The National Association for Music Education.

Farrell, Susan R. *Tools for Powerful Student Evaluation: A Practical Source of Authentic Assessment Strategies for Music Teachers*. Meredith Music Publications.

Hall, Louis O., Nancy R. Boone, John Grashel, and Rosemary C. Watkins, eds. *Strategies for Teaching: Guide for Music Methods Classes*. MENC—The National Association for Music Education.

Hilley, Martha F., and Tommie Pardue, eds. *Strategies for Teaching Middle-Level and High School Keyboard*. MENC—The National Association for Music Education.

Hinckley, June M., and Suzanne M. Shull, eds. *Strategies for Teaching Middle-Level General Music*. MENC—
The National Association for Music Education.

Kvet, Edward L., and Janet M. Tweed, eds. *Strategies for Teaching Beginning and Intermediate Band*. MENC—The National Association for Music Education.

Kvet, Edward J., and John E. Williamson, eds. *Strategies for Teaching High School Band*. MENC—The National Association for Music Education.

Lehman, Paul R. *Aiming for Excellence: The Impact of the Standards Movement on Music Education*. MENC—
The National Association for Music Education.

Lehman, Paul R., ed. *Performance Standards for Music: Strategies and Benchmarks for Assessing Progress toward the National Standards, Grades PreK–12*. MENC—The National Association for Music Education. Available at http://www.menc.org/.

Lehman, Paul R., ed. Teaching Examples: Ideas for Music Educators. MENC—The National Association for Music Education.

Lindeman, Carolynn A. *Benchmarks in Action: A Guide to Standards-Based Assessment in Music. Benchmark Student Performances in Music Series*, edited by Carolynn A. Lindeman. MENC—The National Association for Music Education.

Lindeman, Carolynn A. *Strategies for Teaching Series*. MENC—The National Association for Music Education.

MENC—The National Association for Music Education. *Opportunity-to-Learn Standards for Music Instruction: Grades PreK-12*. Available at www.menc.org.

MENC—The National Association for Music Education. *The School Music Program—A New Vision: The K-12 National Standards, PreK Standards, and What They Mean to Music Educators*. Available at www.menc.org.

Persky, Hilary R., Brent A. Sandene, and Jan M. Askew. Project officer, Sheida White. The NAEP 1997 Arts Report Card, NCES 1999-486. National Center for Education Statistics. Available at http://nces.ed.gov/nationsreportcard/arts/.

Purse, William E., James L. Jordan, and Nancy Marsters, eds. *Strategies for Teaching: Middle-Level and High School Guitar*.

Reese, Sam, Kimberly McCord, and Kimberly Walls, eds. *Strategies for Teaching: Technology*. MENC—The National Association for Music Education.

Reimer, Bennett, ed. *Performing with Understanding: The Challenge of the National Standards for Music Education*. MENC—The National Association for Music Education.

Rinehart, Carroll, ed. *Composing and Arranging: Standard 4 Benchmarks. Benchmark Student Performances in Music Series, edited by Carolynn A. Lindeman*. MENC—The National Association for Music Education.

Sims, Wendy L., ed. *Strategies for Teaching Prekindergarten Music*.

Small, Ann Roberts, and Judy K. Bowers, eds. *Strategies for Teaching Elementary and Middle-Level Chorus*. MENC—The National Association for Music Education.

Stauffer, Sandra L., and Jennifer Davidson, eds. *Strategies for Teaching K–4 General Music*. MENC—The National Association for Music Education.

Straub, Dorothy A., Louis S. Bergonzi, and Anne C. Witt, eds. *Strategies for Teaching Strings and Orchestra*. Available at www.menc.org.

Swiggum, Randal, ed. *Strategies for Teaching High School Chorus*. MENC—The National Association for Music Education.

Thompson, Keith P., and Gloria L. Kiester, eds. *Strategies for Teaching High School General Music*. MENC—
The National Association for Music Education.

Winner, Ellen, Lyle Davidson, and Larry Scripp. *Arts PROPEL: A Music Handbook*. Harvard Project Zero.

Other Resources

Randel, Don Michael. *The New Harvard Dictionary of Music*. Belknap.

Appendix E

Recordings and Printed Music Used in This Study Guide

► ► ► ► ► ► ► ► ► ► ► ►

Recorded Excerpts

Label	Work	Artists	Question Number(s)
London (Decca)	*Concerto for Orchestra*	Béla Bartók; Chicago Symphony, Solti	1
Deutsche Grammophon	*Nocturnes*	Claude Debussy; Cleveland Orchestra, Boulez	2
Music of the World	*Rag Madhur*	Ustad Imrat Kahn, Shafaatullah Kahn	3
Gothic	*Schmücke dich, o liebe Seele*	J. S. Bach; Lippincott	4
Musical Heritage Society	Sonata No. 16, K. 545	W.A. Mozart; Lowy	5, 6
Deutsche Grammophon	Third Symphony	Aaron Copland; New York Philharmonic, Bernstein	7, 8
Hyperion	*O, Jerusalem*	Hildegard von Bingen	9–10
Columbia	You're Blasé	Wynton Marsalis; arr. Freedman	11
Varese Saraband	(Darth Vader Theme)	John Williams; National Philharmonic, Gerhardt	13
Columbia	Jersey Bounce	Les and Larry Elgart	14
Philips	"In wunderschönen Monat Mai"	Robert Schumann	15
Mark	*Syrtos*	Nicholas Roussakis; Rutgers Wind Ensemble, Berz	16
Madacy	Shawnee Stomp Dance		17
Orfeon	"Casa Lupita"	Peres Prado	18
CPO	Four Pieces Op. 15, No. 3	Clara Schumann	20–21
Indiana Univ. Press	Flute Sonata	Anna Amalie	20–21
Rhino	"I Promise to Remember"	Frankie Lyman and the Teenagers	23
Sony	Third Symphony	William Schumann, New York Philharmonic, Bernstein	25

Printed Excerpts, Content Knowledge Practice Test

Publisher	Work	Composer	Question Number(s)
Dover	*Tristan und Isolde*	Richard Wagner	30–31
Dover	*Cosi fan Tutte*	W. A. Mozart	36–37
Dover	String Quartet, K. 465	W. A. Mozart	39

Printed Excerpts, Analysis Practice Test

Publisher	Work	Composer/Arranger	Question Number(s)
Briekopf und Härtel	Quintet in C	Ignaz Pleyel	1
G. Schirmer	*Deep River*	H. Burleigh	2
Warner	Prelude and Fugue in A-flat	J. S. Bach	3A, #1
Southern Music	*Swiss Walking Song*	Reynolds	3A, #2
G. Schirmer	*Fire, Fire My Heart*	Morely/Lincoln	3B, #1
Hal Leonard	*The River*	Audrey Snyder	3B, #2

Appendix F

Response Space for the *Music: Analysis* Test

► ► ► ► ► ► ► ► ► ► ► ►

NO TEST MATERIAL ON THIS PAGE

LAST NAME (first two letters) ☐☐ FIRST INITIAL ☐ TODAY'S DATE ___/___/___

CANDIDATE ID NUMBER ☐☐☐☐☐☐☐☐

SOCIAL SECURITY NUMBER (optional) ☐☐☐ – ☐☐ – ☐☐☐☐

WAIT FOR THE SUPERVISOR'S INSTRUCTIONS BEFORE YOU
OPEN THIS TEST BOOK.

Question 1

Location of Error by Measure Number(s)	Description of Error
1. ____________	____
	____
2. ____________	____
	____
3. ____________	____
	____
4. ____________	____
	____
5. ____________	____
	____

-4-

Question 2

Location of Error by Measure Number(s) | Description of Error

1. ____________ ____

____

2. ____________ ____

____

3. ____________ ____

____

4. ____________ ____

____

5. ____________ ____

____

-5-

Question 3, Topic A: Instrumental Music

Example No. 1

School level (circle one):	elementary	middle/junior high	high school
Ensemble type (circle one):	concert band	jazz band	orchestra

Stylistic influences: ____________________

____

____

____

Performance challenge No. 1: ____________________

____

____

____

Rehearsal technique(s) related to performance challenge No. 1: ____________________

____

____

____

____

____

____

____

____

____

Performance challenge No. 2: ____________________

____

-6-

Question 3, Topic A (continued)

Rehearsal technique(s) related to performance challenge No. 2: ______

Example No. 2

School level (circle one): elementary middle/junior high high school

Ensemble type (circle one): concert band jazz band orchestra

Stylistic influences: ______

Performance challenge No. 1: ______

Question 3, Topic A (continued)

Rehearsal technique(s) related to performance challenge No. 1: ______

Performance challenge No. 2: ______

Rehearsal technique(s) related to performance challenge No. 2: ______

-8-

Question 3, Topic B: Choral Music

Example No. 1

School level (circle one):	elementary	middle/junior high	high school
Ensemble type (circle one):	mixed chorus treble choir	show choir girls' chorus	madrigal/chamber choir boys' choir

Stylistic influences: ______________________________

____

____

____

Performance challenge No. 1: ______________________________

____

____

Rehearsal technique(s) related to performance challenge No. 1: ______________________________

____

____

____

____

____

____

____

____

____

Performance challenge No. 2: ______________________________

____

____

Question 3, Topic B (continued)

Rehearsal technique(s) related to performance challenge No. 2: ______________________

____

____

____

____

____

____

____

____

____

Example No. 2

School level (circle one):	elementary	middle/junior high	high school
Ensemble type (circle one):	mixed chorus treble choir	show choir girls' chorus	madrigal/chamber choir boys' choir

Stylistic influences: ______________________

____

____

____

Performance challenge No. 1: ______________________

____

____

____

____

-10-

Question 3, Topic B (continued)

Rehearsal technique(s) related to performance challenge No. 1: ______

Performance challenge No. 2: ______

Rehearsal technique(s) related to performance challenge No. 2: ______

Question 3, Topic C: General Music

Example No. 1

Grade level (circle one): K–1 2–3 4–5 6–8

Defense of grade-level selection: ____________________

Stylistic influences: ____________________

First concept and how the piece could be used to teach that concept: ____________________

Second concept and how the piece could be used to teach that concept: ____________________

Question 3, Topic C (continued)

Third concept and how the piece could be used to teach that concept:

Example No. 2

Grade level (circle one): K–1 2–3 4–5 6–8

Defense of grade-level selection:

Stylistic influences:

First concept and how the piece could be used to teach that concept:

-13-

Question 3, Topic C (continued)

Second concept and how the piece could be used to teach that concept:

Third concept and how the piece could be used to teach that concept: